the mikaere foundation

the nkh charity cookbook

2022

ISBN: 978-1-915064-41-7

Dedicated to all our NKH bees. Hold tight loves, we're working towards a cure for you! x

This Mikaere Foundation is not responsible for the outcome of any recipe you try from this book. You may not achieve the results desired due to variations in ingredients, cooking temperatures, typos, errors, omissions, or individual cooking ability. You should always use your best judgement when cooking with raw ingredients such as eggs, chicken or fish and seek expert advice before beginning if you are unsure. You should always take care not to injure yourself or others on sharp knives or other cooking implements or to burn yourself or others while cooking. You should examine the contents of ingredients prior to preparation and consumption of these recipes in order to be fully aware of and to accurately advise others of the presence of substances which might provoke an adverse reaction in some consumers. Recipes available in this book may not have been formally tested by us or for us and we do not provide any assurances nor accept any responsibility or liability with regard to their originality, efficacy, quality, or safety.

Many thanks to the NKH community and everyone who submitted a recipe.
Many thanks to both Sam and Wendy Hulance for their proofreading skills. <3

Collated with love in the UK.
This cookbook has been printed on demand just for you.

CONTENTS

the mikaere foundation

HELLO!

Glycine Encephalopathy/Nonketotic Hyperglycinemia is a rare and terminal metabolic disorder. It's hard to explain what living with NKH is like, as a parent. It's not what we expected. There is a lot more heartache and grief than we'd like. No one wants to see their child live an incredibly medicalised life, miss milestones and suffer ongoing pain. Add the ableism we face raising disabled kids and the general lack of accessibility in the world, we love our kids but it can be difficult. Even more so when children with NKH have limited life expectancies. Many, many children have died before we were ready for them to.

But, we have hope in a cure. Because NKH is so rare, there is little to no awareness. There is not a lot of funding for research. So we, as parents fund what we can. Through local fundraisers, events and raffles. And charity cookbooks. This book supports The Mikaere Foundation. Every single penny raised from the royalties of this cookbook will go towards NKH Research, to better understand the disorder and discover effective treatments, such as gene replacement therapy. We have hope.

Thank you so much to all who submitted a recipe for this book, to the wider NKH community for being so supportive, and to you, for purchasing a copy. Thanks for helping fund a cure for our children.

ABOUT MIKAERE AND THE MIKAERE FOUNDATION

Mikaere was born with Nonketotic Hyperglycinemia in October 2016. Mikaere, Elly and Sam spent countless weeks in Intensive Care, hospital and hospice on end of life care. We're lucky to currently be home with our little guy. He's well-loved, but living with NKH is not what we expected. We were determined that our little boy would make his mark on this world and wanted to contribute to the NKH community that has supported our little family, and so founded the Mikaere Foundation, a registered charity in England and Wales (Charity number 1200720). Since Mikaere's birth, we have raised over £250,000+ for NKH research and have hope that one day soon an effective treatment will be available for kids with NKH.

Thanks so much for being here, we appreciate you!

Love, The Hulance Family x

www.mikaerefoundation.org

APPETISERS, SOUPS AND SALADS

ANNA'S CHEESY SPINACH AND ARTICHOKE DIP

APPETISER

DIRECTIONS

1. Preheat oven to 180 °C/350 °F.
2. Defrost the spinach and squeeze as much water out as you can, by pushing it down between a sieve and a bowl, and patting between kitchen roll/paper towels.
3. Place spinach, cream cheese, artichoke hearts, grated cheddar and sour cream into a bowl, and mix well.
4. Place into oven safe serving dish and sprinkle on grated parmesan.
5. Bake for 20 minutes at 180 °C/350 °F until it's bubbling and crispy on top.
6. Serve with pita slices, crisps, sliced baguette or veggie sticks.

Serves 6-8

30 minutes

Recipe contributed from
Boston, USA, via Laura Gates (UK)

INGREDIENTS

375g/13oz frozen spinach

400g/14oz can of artichoke hearts, diced

280g/9.5oz cream cheese

250g/9oz grated cheddar cheese

4-5 tablespoons sour cream

80g/3oz grated parmesan

NOTES

If you are not into cheddar, you can substitute with mozzarella, or use a mix of both! If the dip is a bit thick, you can add a bit more sour cream till it's your desired consistency.

ABOUT

This is an absolute winner of an appetiser, or as a side dish. A very dear, old friend of mine (Anna) used to make it for us whenever we went round for supper club. She used to say "Guys, not again!" but we all love it so much we would plead and beg! Then we'd all fill ourselves up too much with it and not be able to finish supper! Absolutely gorgeous, just like Anna!

BUFFALO CHICKEN DIP

APPETISER

INGREDIENTS

2 cups cooked, shredded chicken

250ml/8oz cream cheese, softened

250ml/8oz ranch dressing

1 (360ml/12 oz) bottle of Franks Red Hot

1.5 cups shredded cheddar cheese

Tortilla chips, for serving

Serves 4-6

Approx 35 minutes

Recipe contributed from the USA by Tanya Graves

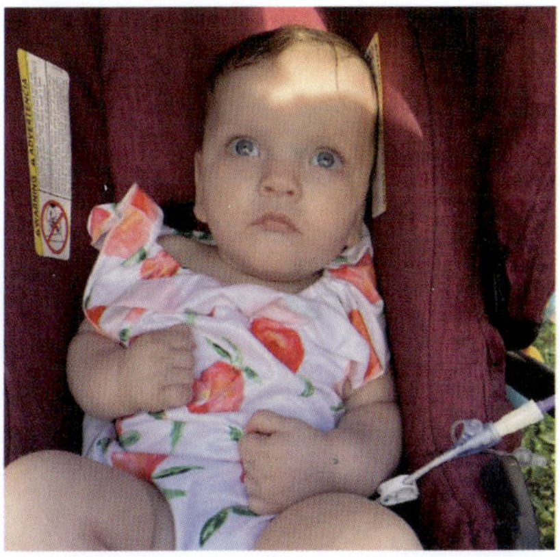

DIRECTIONS

1. In a pot, heat chicken and Red Hot until heated through.
2. Stir in cream cheese and Ranch dressing, stirring well until blended and warm.
3. Mix in half the cheddar cheese, and stir.
4. Transfer to a slow cooker.
5. Sprinkle remaining cheese over top.
6. Cover and cook on low until hot and bubbly.
7. Serve with Tortilla Chips.

NOTES

You can use leftovers, canned chicken or rotisserie chicken. If you don't have a slowcooker, transfer to an oven safe dish and bake in the oven 190 °C/375 °F until the cheese is bubbly.

ABOUT

This recipe was contributed by Ezmerae's Nay Nay. Ezmerae is a sweet eleven month old who has NKH. Every day is a challenge, but at the end of each day, it is all worth every moment.

HOMEMADE PICO DE GULLO

APPETISER

INGREDIENTS

4-6 large, ripe tomatoes

1 lime

1 bunch of coriander/cilantro

1 small red onion

Serves 4-6

10 minutes

Recipe contributed from the UK

DIRECTIONS

1. Dice the tomato into pieces, the size of your little fingernail.
2. Dice the onion to similar size.
3. Pick the leaves off the stalks of the coriander, and chop.
4. Add to the tomatoes.
5. Add the juice of one lime.
6. Season with salt and pepper, and mix well.
7. Let rest for 10 minutes before serving.

NOTES

Fresh tomatoes are key! This is a very verstatile recipe. You can add capsicum/peppers, or even jalapeños, if you like it hot. The trick is to chop everything very finely and to mix well. It can be served with tortilla chips, or on practically anything. Quesadillas, burritos, tacos, eggs etc.

HOMEMADE GUACOMOLE

APPETISER

DIRECTIONS

1. Halve the avocados and remove the pit. Scoop into a bowl.
2. Mash with a fork till it's your preferred consistency. Add the remaining ingredients, and mix.
3. Season with salt and pepper.
4. Taste test, and add more lime juice/salt if needed.
5. Serve with Tortilla chips.

NOTES

Definitely use fresh lime, not lime juice. Roma tomatoes are less watery, which is ideal in guacomole, but you can use other tomatoes in a pinch. Add Jalapeño's if you like it hot. To keep your leftover guac green, add to airtight container, and smoosh with a spoon until it's flat. Add a half inch of water, and store in fridge. Will last around 3 days without going brown!

Serves 2-4

10 minutes

Recipe contributed from the UK

INGREDIENTS

3 ripe but firm avocados

1/2 small onion, diced

2 small diced roma tomatoes

1 lime, juiced

1 bunch of coriander/cilantro, stalks discarded, leaves finely diced

SMOKED MACKEREL PÂTÉ

APPETISER

INGREDIENTS

165g/6oz smoked mackerel fillets

200g/7oz cream cheese

1 lemon

1 very small bunch fresh flat-leaf parsley or chives

Bread, baguette or cracker breads, for serving

Serves 4-6

10 minutes

Recipe contributed from the UK

DIRECTIONS

1. Peel the skin off the smoked mackerel and discard.
2. Ensure there are no bones in the fillet, break up the fish and add to bowl.
3. Add the cream cheese.
4. Add the zest and most of the juice of a lemon.
5. Pick a few leaves from the parsley, chop finely and add to the mix.
6. Use a fork to mix together, until it's well combined and very rustic looking. Season to taste.
7. Decant to a serving dish, garnish with more chives/parsley and serve with breads.

ABOUT

This recipe was contributed by Elly, Mikaere's Mama. Mikaere is 6, from London, UK and lives with NKH. He's so loved, so very very loved. You can follow us on instagram at @teammikaere.

NOTES

You can use a food processer or blender to get a smoother pâté, if you please. But it's more rustic and there is less faff and washing up if you do it in a bowl. This is one my favourite snacky things to serve, it's so simple, delicious and we've had such nice compliments about it! After trying it, one of our friends went home and made himself a batch!

FRENCH CHICKEN PÂTÉ

APPETISER

INGREDIENTS

225g/8oz chicken liver

75g/2.7oz unsalted butter

2 cloves garlic, minced

125ml/half cup water

1 medium, minced shallot

2 tablespoons double/heavy cream

1 sprig fresh thyme leaves (stalk removed)

1/2 teaspoon each salt + black pepper

Serves 4-6

Approx 40 minutes

Recipe contributed from New Zealand

DIRECTIONS

1. Trim any white connective tissue from the chicken livers.

2. Melt a tablespoon of butter in a skillet over medium heat and add the minced garlic and shallots. Cook for a minute, until fragrant.

4. Add the chicken livers, salt, black pepper, thyme leaves and water. Turn up the heat and bring to simmer.

5. Reduce heat to low and cover. Simmer for 5-8 minutes, stirring occasionally, until the livers are a light brown, and barely pink on the inside. Turn off the heat, and leave the livers covered in the pan for 5 min.

6. Drain the liquid from the pan and transfer to a blender or food processer. Blend, gradually adding the cream and remaining butter. Blend in additional salt/pepper to taste.

8. Transfer paté to ramekins or glass jars, and cover with plastic wrap touching the paté (so no air can get in).

9. Refrigerate overnight (or at least 4-5 hours) until firm.

10. Serve with warm, crusty bread/oatcakes, or on crackers with a side salad with a drizzle of balsamic vinegar/olive oil. It also goes really well with red onion marmalade (see page 106 for the recipe).

NOTES

if you'd prefer a more traditional recipe, you can subsitute the water for a good quality brandy. If you'd prefer a keto version, you can substitute the double cream for coconut cream and the butter for ghee.

GRILLED CHEESE ROLL UPS

APPETISER

INGREDIENTS

8-10 Slices of very fresh white, thick sandwich bread

150g/5oz of finely grated cheddar cheese

2 tablespoons melted butter

Serves 2-3

30 minutes

Recipe contributed from Scotland

DIRECTIONS

1. Lay bread on chopping board and slice off crusts.
2. Use a rolling pin to roll each slice flat.
3. Sprinkle over cheese, leaving a gap at the top.
4. Starting at the cheese end, tightly (but gently) roll the slice until you get to the gap.
5. Brush the gap with butter, and gently pat to close.
6. Brush the outside with butter on all sides.
7. Place in a non-stick pan over low medium heat, seam side down.
8. Fry until golden, turning frequently to ensure an even colour.
9. Serve with soup, or with runny eggs. Good for dunking!

NOTES

It's important to use soft white sandwich bread. Avoid firm breads (like sourdough) or seeded breads as they won't roll properly. Other melty cheeses are good too, such as Gruyere or shredded Mozzarella. We've tried with Marmite (which was great), and with thin crispy bacon. We also like it with pesto if you're feeling fancy!

- Jess Watson

RUTH'S BACON CURLIEWHIRLIES

APPETISER

INGREDIENTS

1 sheet puff pastry

1 packet streaky bacon

milk, to brush

Serves 4-6

5 min prep, 30 min + cooling, 15 min cooking

Recipe contributed from New Zealand, via the UK

DIRECTIONS

1. Heat the oven to 180 °C/375 °F (with fan).
2. Roll out your pastry sheet.
3. Lay the bacon strips all the way along the sheet, leaving a small gap at the edge.
4. Brush the edge with cold water.
5. Starting opposite to the edge, roll the sheet as tightly as you can.
6. Use your fingers to seal up the join.
7. Refrigerate for at least 30 mins - the longer the better.
8. Remove the roll, and brush milk over the top.
9. Slice thinly with a sharp knife, and put the slices on a greased tray.
10. Bake in the oven for 10-15 minutes, until the pastry is golden.
11. Cool on a wire rack, and serve.

ABOUT

I imagine lots of families have versions of this snack, and my mum has been making these for years and years. They've starred at 21sts, weddings, and every family gathering. They're really easy to make, even easier to eat, and people are always happy to see them - Emma Coley.

NOTES

The longer they chill, the easier they are to cut. I like to make them the morning of a party, chill all day, and slice and cook them late in the afternoon. Best fresh, but if they're stored in an airtight container once cool, they can be served the next day. Make them veggie with a thin layer of pesto and parmesan, or sweet chilli sauce.

CHEESYMITE SCROLLS

APPETISER

INGREDIENTS

2 cups self raising flour

90g/3.2oz chopped and chilled unsalted butter

150ml milk

2 tablespoons extra butter

5 tablespoons Marmite

80g/3oz grated cheddar cheese

Makes 16 scrolls

60 minutes

Recipe contributed from New Zealand

NOTES

While not the original from Bakers Delight, it's still a pretty good imitation. Our family LOVES these, and we rarely have leftovers. The trick is to be sparing with the marmite and be generous with the cheese. It's best on the same day (ideally still warm) but is good for picnics when cold, too. You can cut the rectangle in half long ways for mini scrolls, and bake for 5 minutes less.

DIRECTIONS

1. Preheat the oven to 200°C/390 °F (fan bake. Heat to 220°C/430 °F if using a conventional oven).
2. Line a 23cm round baking tin with baking paper, and grease.
3. Sift the self-raising flour into a bowl. Add chilled butter and rub into the flour until the mixture resembles breadcrumbs.
4. Add the milk and mix gently until the mixture forms a dough.
6. Knead the dough, on a lightly floured cutting board, until smooth, and dough is elastic when stretched.
7. Roll the dough into a long rectangle, about 1 cm thick.
8. Spread the butter and then the Marmite over dough, leaving a small border.
9. Sprinkling the cheese over the Marmite.
10. Starting from the long edge of the rectangle, roll the dough firmly into a log.
11. Using a sharp knife, cut the roll into 3-4 cm slices.
12. Place the slices, cut side up, into the prepared tin.
13. Bake for 15-20 minutes or until golden. The scrolls will sound hollow when tapped once baked.
14. Leave the scrolls to cool in the tin for 10 minutes. Transfer to a wire rack to cool completely.

PIZZA SCROLLS

APPETISER

DIRECTIONS

1. Tip the bread mix into a bowl and stir in the dried herbs.
2. Add the oil then gradually add about 300ml warm water to make the dough.
3. Knead on a lightly floured surface for 5-7 minutes until smooth. Place in an oiled bowl, cover, and leave to rise for 1 hour or until doubled in size.
4. Knock the dough back in the bowl, then tip out onto a floured surface and roll out to a rectangle about 20 x 30cm. Spread the pasta sauce over the dough, leaving a narrow border all around the edge.
5. Mix the mozzarella and Parmesan together and scatter about two-thirds of the cheese all over the dough.
6. Scatter on chopped roasted peppers then arrange the pepperoni slices on top.
7. Roll up from one of the short sides, like a Swiss roll, and pinch the seam closed.
8. Cut into 8 thick slices and arrange cut-side up in a lined baking tin (about 20 x 30cm), quite close together but not touching.
9. Cover and leave to prove for 30 minutes. Preheat the oven to 180°C/390°F (fan bake. Heat to 220 °C/430 °F if using a conventional oven, or gas mark 6).
10. Uncover the pizza rolls once they have proved and bake for 15 minutes initially.
11. Scatter the rest of the cheese and the sesame seeds over the top and bake for a further 15 minutes or until golden and cooked through. Leave to cool for at least 15-20 minutes before serving.

Serves 4-6

70 minutes

Recipe contributed from Australia

INGREDIENTS

500g/17.5oz pack white bread mix

1 teaspoon dried mixed herbs

1 tablespoon olive oil

flour for dusting

150g/5.30z tomato + herb pasta sauce

150g/5.30z shredded mozzarella

40g/1.5oz finely grated Parmesan

2 roasted peppers, chopped

100g/3.5oz sliced pepperoni

1 teaspoon sesame seeds

THE BITSY GRAZING BOARD

APPETISER

INGREDIENTS

2-3 different cheeses, of various types (Smoked cheddar, Gouda, Goats, Brie, Comté, Gruyère, Manchego)

2-3 different fruits (grapes, berries, pears, dried apricots, strawberries, melon - whatever is in season)

A selection of nuts (roasted and smoked is fun)

2-3 different kinds of cheese vehicles (breads, baguettes, crackers, breadsticks, crisps etc)

A selection of deli meats (salami, pastrami, chicken bits, salmon or ham, prawns etc)

2-3 different kinds of veggies (carrot or capsicum sticks, cucmber slices, cherry tomatoes, olives, sliced avocado etc)

1 tub of high quality hummus

A selection of chutneys, or chilli jam

Anything else you have on hand (pasta salad, egg mayo, coronation chicken etc) or anything from the deli section (scotch eggs, mini quiches etc)

Serves 4-6

Approx 15 minutes

Recipe contributed from the UK

DIRECTIONS

This recipe is more about assembling, than cooking. The trick is to make sure everything is bite sized, and easy to eat. Gather your platters (we like to use wooden cutting boards) and assemble on the boards, mixing everything up a little. Make sure everything is decanted and there are no plastic containers or wrapping to take away from the aesthetics.

Tip: Fill any holes or spaces with fruit.

ROAST TOMATO TART

APPETISER

DIRECTIONS

1. Slice your tomatoes crosswise, along their hemisphere.
2. Line a large baking sheet with paper towels. Set the sliced tomatoes on top in a single layer.
3. In a small bowl, combine the salt and pepper. Season the tomatoes evenly on both sides, cover with another paper towel and let sit, 15 minutes, allowing the salt to draw moisture out of the tomatoes.
4. As the tomatoes sit, heat the oven to 200 °C/400 °F and set a rack in the middle of the oven, and place an empty backing sheet upside down on the rack.
5. Roll out the puff pastry into a 22x28cm/9x11-inch rectangle, trimming any uneven edges. Prick the inside with a fork every few cms, leaving a 1.5cm/½-inch border.
6. Brush the center of the puff pastry with the crème fraîche, leaving the border unbrushed.
7. Layer the tomatoes and red onion on top of the tart, within the border, allowing them to overlap slightly.
8. Transfer to a sheet pan and place on the upside down baking sheet in the oven.
9. Bake, rotating halfway through, until puff pastry is browned and puffed, around 30 to 35 minutes.
10. Allow to cool slightly, for 5-10 minutes or so.
11. Dollop with fresh ricotta.
12. Thin pesto with olive oil until it reaches the proper consistency for drizzling; drizzle on top of tart to taste.
13. Top with basil and pepper flakes, if using, and serve.

Serves 4

60 minutes

Recipe contributed from the UK

INGREDIENTS

6 medium, multicoloured tomatoes (about 340g/12oz in total)

1 teaspoon salt

1 teaspoon black pepper

1 sheet packaged puff pastry, thawed

3 tablespoons crème fraîche

¾ cup fresh ricotta

Pesto, for drizzling

Extra-virgin olive oil, for drizzling

Fresh basil leaves, for garnish (optional)

Red-pepper flakes, for garnish (optional)

NOTES

This tart is super light and DELICIOUS! Good for smaller, sturdy tomatoes (like heirloom or campari, not the giant, about-to-burst kind). You can sub the crème fraîche for sour cream in a pinch, but don't skip it.. Definitely salt the tomatoes - it helps prevent a soggy crust and zings everything up. If you're feeling adventurous, change it up by adding parmesean cheese, sliced olives or toasted pine nuts.

HEIRLOOM TOMATO QUICHE

APPETISER

Serves 4-6

60 minutes, plus
90 min chill time

Recipe contributed
from the UK

INGREDIENTS

FOR THE CRUST

160g/1 ¼ cup all-purpose flour

¼ teaspoon fine sea salt

140g/10 tablespoons unsalted butter, cold and cut into cubes

3-4 tablespoons ice water, as needed

FOR THE QUICHE

1 ½lb/650g ripe heirloom tomatoes (about 4 medium sized tomatoes)

¼ cup cup pesto

¾ cup/85g/3oz shredded mozzarella

1 tablespoon finely chopped fresh basil

1 tablespoon finely chopped fresh oregano

3 large eggs

⅓ cup double/heavy cream

½ teaspoon kosher salt

½ teaspoon freshly ground black pepper

DIRECTIONS

1. In a large bowl, whisk together the flour and salt to combine.
2. Add the butter, tossing the cubes through the flour until the pieces are separated from one another and each piece is coated.
3. Cut the butter into the flour by pressing the pieces between your palms or fingertips, flattening the cubes into big shards and continuing to toss them in the flour to recoat the shards. Stop when the butter pieces are about the size of walnut halves.
4. Make a well in the center of the mixture. Add 3 tablespoons ice water and mix it in by tossing the flour in the bowl. (This tossing movement lets the moisture incorporate without allowing too much gluten formation.)
5. Continue to add ice water 1 to 2 tablespoons at a time until the dough begins to come together. As it comes together, fold it over itself a few times to make sure it's homogenous.
6. The dough should hold together with some cracks, but not large, noticeable cracks (a sign of underhydration), but it should not be wet or tacky to the touch (a sign of overhydration).
7. Form the dough into a disk about 1-inch thick. Wrap tightly in plastic wrap and refrigerate for at least 90 minutes before using, and up to 2 days. (It can also be frozen for up to 3 months, then thawed overnight before using.)
8. When ready to make the tart, heat oven to 180 °C/350 °F degrees.
9. Cut the tomatoes into 1½cm/½ inch slices and salt generously. Place on paper towels to drain. Cover with paper towel when done, and leave for 20 minutes.

DIRECTIONS CONT

10. Roll out the dough to a 28cm/11inch circle, and fit into a 23cm/9 inch tart pan, allowing the edges to rise just a bit over the edge of the pan. Prick the dough all over with a fork.
11. Line the dough with aluminum foil and fill with pie weights or dried beans. Bake for 15 minutes until beginning to brown at the edges.
12. Remove from the oven and carefully remove the foil and weights, and allow to cool. Increase the oven temperature to 190 °C/375 °F.
13. In a medium bowl, prepare the custard: Whisk together the eggs, cream, salt and pepper until combined.
14. Spread pesto in an even layer over the parbaked tart crust. Sprinkle the shredded mozzarella over the pesto. Sprinkle the fresh basil and oregano over the cheese.
15. Pour the custard evenly over the base. Swirl the pan to evenly distribute the liquid.
16. Place the sliced tomatoes evenly over the custard in overlapping concentric circles.
17. Bake until the filling is just set and won't jiggle when shaken, about 35-45 minutes.
18. Remove from the oven and let it rest for 20 minutes to firm up.
19. Garnish with basil leaves before before serving.

NOTES

Such a lovely recipe, one of our favourites! You can easily use storebought pie crust if you don't fancy making your own, a great shortcut for weeknight meals, and the tart crust can be parbaked a day in advance. If you'd prefer a slightly lighter quiche, you can substiute the double cream for Carnation Evaporated Milk. You can also roast the tomatoes for 10-15 minutes to dry out some of the juice, the less juicy they are, the less likely you are to have a soggy bottom on the tart. If you don't like the look of the tomatoes on top, you can switch steps 15 + 16, add them to the base and swirl the custard on top.

CORN FRITTERS

APPETISER

DIRECTIONS

1. Boil the corn as per packet instructions (or use fresh, boil the cobs, and cut off the kernels once cooked). Drain well.
2. Beat the eggs and the milk in a large bowl.
3. Finely cut the spring onions, and add them with the sweetcorn to the egg mix.
4. Sift the the flour, baking powder, salt, pepper and paprika into the bowl, and stir until combined.
5. Heat oil in a frying pan, and drop tablespoons of batter into the pan. Cook until the fritters are bubbling to the top and the base is golden, then flip.
6. Drain on paper towels.
7. Serve with Crème Fraîche, and chopped chives.

NOTES

This is a kiwi breakfast classic, and is super versatile. You can use canned corn, drained well if it's easier. You can also used creamed corn (though omit two eggs, if you do). You can also serve it with poached eggs, or tomato salsa. It's wildly versatile!

Serves 2

30 minutes

Recipe contributed from the NZ

INGREDIENTS

400g frozen sweetcorn

3 spring onions

3 eggs

2 tablespoons/30ml milk

¾ cup/75g plain white flour

1 teaspoon baking powder

½ teaspoon salt

pinch of black pepper

pinch of paprika

Oil, for frying

Dollop of crème fraîche

1-2 strands of chives, for garnish

ARNZ'S FRIED BREAD

APPETISER

Serves 2

60 minutes

Recipe contributed from the NZ

DIRECTIONS

1. In a large bowl, add the 6 cups of flour, and make a well in the centre.
2. Sprinkle 4 teaspoons of sure bake yeast over the flour.
3. Add 1 tablespoon of oil and ½ teaspoon of salt to the well.
4. Pour in 3 cups of warm water, and mix from the middle out. Ideally it should be wet enough to use all the flour in the bowl, but don't worry if it's too wet.
4. Leave it to rise for half an hour.
5. Punch it down, and work it till you can roll it out.
6. Roll it out into a puffy rectangle, and leave for another 20 minutes.
7. Add oil to a frying pan (enough that it's an inch/2.5cm deep), enough for a shallow fry, and heat.
8. Cut the dough into squares 5cm/2inches across, and fry until golden brown. Place on a paper towel, and cover to keep warm while you cook the rest.
9. Serve warm!

INGREDIENTS

6 cups white plain flour

4 teaspoons surebake yeast

1 tablespoon oil

2 cups oil, for frying

½ teaspoon salt

3 cups warm water

NOTES

Surebake yeast is different to active dry yeast, and instant yeast - it's formulated especially for breadmakers and contains a mix of active dry yeast and bread improvers (such as wheat flour and sugar) which means there is a lower concentration of yeast in the jar. For those outside New Zealand, you can substitue with a breadmaker yeast, or in a pinch, active dry yeast. If you would like them sweet add 6 tablespoons of sugar (or a bit more if you like them doughnut sweet).

ABOUT

Arnz is the cousin of Elly's best friend, Liz. Arnz made these at Liz's wedding, and Elly stood by the fryer eating them as they came out of the pan. Genuinely one of my most favourite food memories!

NO BUTTER CHEESE SCONES

APPETISER

DIRECTIONS

1. Preheat the oven and baking tray to 200°C/395°F
2. Mix all dry ingredients and stir in 95% of the grated cheese.
3. Mix in the milk. When just mixed together, turn onto a floured surface and knead for 5 or so minutes (not too much, you don't want to over knead it).
4. Shape into a rectangle, approximately 2.5cm/1inch high and slice into squares (8-12 depending on size you want).
5. Sprinkle the remaining cheese on top.
6. Transfer to the hot tray and bake in middle of oven for 15-20 minutes.
7. Stand for 10 min before eating.

Serves 8-12

20 minutes prep + cooling
20 minutes baking

Recipe contributed from Aoeteroa/New Zealand

INGREDIENTS

2 cups standard/all purpose flour

2 heaped teaspoons baking powder

1 heaped teaspoon finely ground rock salt

1 teaspoon white sugar

2 cups tasty cheese (a mature cheddar)

1 cup blue milk (whole milk/full fat)

NOTES

Mixed Herbs can be a tasty addition, (add 2 teaspoons to the dry ingredients), as can a teaspoon of ground Cayenne pepper.

ABOUT

Recipe submitted by Andrew Day, a good friend of Elly and Sam. This recipe (or similar) was originally on the Chelsea Sugar website. Andrew has adapted it slightly.

LIGHT FISH CHOWDER

SOUP

DIRECTIONS

1. Warm the olive oil in a large pot over medium heat and sauté garlic and half of the celery stalks until fragrant. Meanwhile, roughly chop 5 of the carrots (makes roughly 3 cups). Add the carrots, white wine and 3 cups of the stock to the pot and bring to a boil.
2. Lower heat and simmer for 5-6 minutes, or until carrots are very soft.
3. Remove pot from heat. Blend until smooth with an immersion blender or in batches with a countertop blender. If needed, add some of the remaining 1 cup stock to thin soup to desired consistency. Taste and add a little salt if needed.
4. Return pot to stove and bring back to a simmer. Meanwhile, dice remaining carrot and celery into small, bite sized pieces. Add to the blended soup.
5. Simmer for 10 minutes, or so, until it's all soft. Add the fish, peas and courgette and simmer for 5 minutes more, or until fish is cooked through.
6. Add shellfish, and wait a minute to warm through.
7. Taste and add a little vinegar for brightness.
8. Garnish each serving with chopped parsley.

Serves 4-6

45 minutes

Recipe contributed from the UK

INGREDIENTS

1 tablespoon olive oil

¼ cup of white wine

½ teaspoon white wine vinegar

1L stock (chicken, fish or vegetable)

500g/1lb of fish (white fish works well, but also salmon, smoked hake are good alternatives, or use a mix!)

250g/9oz precooked shell fish (prawns, mussels, calamari etc)

1 clove garlic, minced

2 stalks of celery

6 carrots

1 courgette

½ cup peas

Chopped fresh parsley, for garnish

NOTES

This is a great low-carb, dairy free alternative to your regular rich, dairy-based chowder. It's super delicious, very light but still filling. If you prefer, you can substitute some of the carrots in the base for potatoes, for a slightly creamier, less orange base.

VEGAN THAI COCONUT RED LENTIL
SOUP

DIRECTIONS

1. Heat the oil in a large pot over medium heat. Add the onion and carrot and cook 5 minutes, or until softened.
2. Stir in the garlic, tomato paste, curry paste and cayenne and cook until fragrant, about 1 minute.
3. Add the lentils, 1 teaspoon salt and the water. Bring to a simmer, then turn the heat down to medium-low. Partially cover the pan and cook 20 minutes, until the lentils have swelled and softened and the mixture is thickened.
4. Remove from the heat and stir in the coconut milk and lime juice. Taste and season with additional salt if you like.
5. Serve in bowls garnished with coriander.

NOTES

Blend with an immersion stick blender to partially puree, if you'd prefer a smoother soup. For a more robust soup, throw in 1/2 cup of potatoes with the carrots. You can also add baby spinach leaves too! If you're not vegan, add a spoonful of greek yoghurt to make it fancy before you garnish and serve.

Serves 4-6

35 minutes

Recipe contributed from New Zealand - Thanks Carrie Callaghan!

INGREDIENTS

1 cup red lentils

2 tablespoons coconut oil

1 tablespoon minced garlic

3 tablespoons tomato paste

3 tablespoons fresh lime juice

⅓ cup thai red curry paste

¼ teaspoon cayene pepper

1 cup full fat coconut milk

1 cup fresh coriander/cilantro leaves

1 large chopped onion

2 chopped carrots

1L Water

PRAWN WONTON
SOUP

Serves 2-3

90 minutes

Recipe contributed from the UK

INGREDIENTS

WONTONS

300grams uncooked prawns, peeled, deveined + roughly chopped

1 tablespoon chopped coriander/cilantro

1 spring onion/scallion, thinly sliced

1½ teaspoon finely diced ginger

1 teaspoon Shaoxing wine

1 teaspoon light soy sauce

¼ teaspoon white sugar

¼ teaspoon sesame oil

16 square wonton wrappers

BROTH

750ml/25.4oz chicken broth

2 garlic cloves, crushed

1cm piece of ginger, thinly sliced

1½ teaspoon light soy sauce

1 teaspoon sugar

1½ teaspoon Shaoxing wine

¼ - ½ teaspoon sesame oil

2 bok choy, trimmed, cut crossways into 4

2 spring onions/scallions, thinly sliced

DIRECTIONS

1. For wontons, combine all ingredients except wrappers in a bowl, cover and chill for 30 minutes to marinate. Working with a few wrappers at a time, keeping remaining covered with a tea towel, place heaped teaspoonfuls of prawn mixture in the centre of each, dampen edges with a little water, then fold over to form a triangle and press edges to push out any air and seal. Lightly dampen one corner with water, then bring the two ends together with a twisting action, pressing lightly to join. Place on a tray lined with baking paper and cover while you make remaining wontons.
2. Bring stock to the boil in a large saucepan. Add garlic, ginger, soy, shaoxing wine, sugar and sesame oil, reduce to a simmer. Add wontons and simmer for 2 minutes, then add bok choy and simmer until bright green and wontons are cooked through (approx 1-2 minutes – to test, cut through a wonton with a sharp knife).
3. Divide soup, wontons and bok choy among bowls, scatter with spring onion and serve hot.

(EVERY) SATURDAY TUNA CHOWDER

SOUP

INGREDIENTS

25g butter or vegetable oil

1 medium onion, finely chopped

1 fish or chicken stock cube, dissolved in

150ml boiling water

200g can of tuna

200g tin of sweetcorn

pinch of cayenne pepper

1 teaspoon parsley, dried or fresh

600ml milk

2 heaped dessert spoons cornflour

NOTES

You can increase the amount of cornflour for a thicker chowder or add more milk for a thinner chowder.

Serves 4

Recipe contributed from Toddington, UK

20 minutes

DIRECTIONS

1. Melt the butter (or heat the oil) add onion and fry gently for 3 minutes.
2. On medium heat, add cayenne pepper, tuna with any liquid from the tin, sweetcorn and stock.
3. Mix cornflour with some of the milk to form a paste, then add this to the pan with the remaining milk.
4. Increase the heat, stirring constantly, until thickened, then add the parsley.
5. Simmer on gentle heat for 5 minutes until heated through.
6. Serve with grated cheese on top with fresh bread for dunking!

ABOUT

Recipe submitted by The Collins family, who said It has become a family staple - cheap, quick and easy to prepare, and delicious!

BROCCOLI SOUP WITH GINGER + LEMON

SOUP

Serves 4

30 minutes

Recipe contributed from New Zealand - Thanks Carrie Callaghan!

INGREDIENTS

1 tablespoon toasted (dark) sesame oil

4 cloves of garlic, chopped

4 green onions, roughly chopped

5cm/2inch piece of fresh ginger, peeled and chopped

4 cups roughly chopped broccoli (florets and some stems)

4 cups water, divided

4 packed cups pre-washed baby spinach leaves

1 teaspoon fine sea salt

2 tablespoons fresh lemon juice

2 tablespoon sriracha or hot sauce/ pepper of choice

Optional: toasted sesame seeds, additional sriracha, additional sesame oil. If you're not vegan, a dollop of greek yoghurt can work well, too.

DIRECTIONS

1. In a large saucepan, heat the sesame oil over medium heat. Add the garlic, green onions, and ginger; cook and stir for 1-2 minutes.
2. Add the broccoli and 1 cup of the water. Increase heat to medium-high, cover, and cook for 1 minute.
3. Add the spinach, re-cover, and cook 1 minute longer or until spinach is just wilted. Remove pan from heat and let stand, covered, for 5 minutes.
4. Transfer the contents of the pan, along with 1 cup remaining water, to a blender. Puree until smooth, then return mixture to pan.
5. Whisk the remaining water, salt, lemon juice, and sriracha into the soup (add more water if too thick). Reheat over medium-low heat until hot, about 5 minutes. Adjust the salt and pepper to taste.
6. If desired, serve sprinkled with sesame seeds and drizzled with a dollop of greek yoghurt if you fancy.

THAI-ISH NOODLE
SOUP

INGREDIENTS

2 400ml tins of nice coconut milk

1 pint/16oz of chicken stock

4 pieces white fish (basa, cod, whatever is cheap), fresh or frozen

8 pieces frozen gyoza

4 nests of dried noodles

1 x 190ml pot of jar of red thai curry paste (something mild like massaman, or laksa paste)

A splash of stir fry oil, sesame oil, or olive oil depending on what you have to hand

Miscellaneous vegetables (Any other yummy crunchy veg you have lying around - you can mix it up but I'd suggest tenderstem broccoli, asparagus and spring onions)

2 fistfuls of frozen broad beans

1 pack baby sweetcorn

1 pack sugarsnap peas

1 long red pepper/capsicum (or sweet red pepper)

Sesame seeds to garnish

Minced ginger + minced garlic, to your taste

NOTES

This is a quick one! And it works well with whatever veg is in-season. I'd suggest the baby sweetcorn and sugarsnap peas are essentials, but they can be dear depending on the time of year so they'll happily change out for something sweeter. With the mix of frozen ingredients and seasonal veg it can be quite a cheap, but extravagant looking meal to prep. If your baby sweetcorn are thicker than a finger, you may want to cut them in half - to make sure they blanch properly and are tasty crunchy, rather than like eating railroad spikes.

You'll need a timer!

DIRECTIONS

This is a low prep recipe, rejoice! Before we cook:

1. Pop a pan of lightly salted water on to boil for your noodles. Bring a larger pan to medium heat with a small splash of oil.
2. Dump two fistfuls of frozen broad beans, your baby sweetcorn, sugar snap peas and any other crunchy green veg in to a large glass or ceramic bowl.
3. Fry your ginger and garlic for a moment to soften them, and then lightly toast two to three heaped dessert spoons of your red curry paste in the larger pan for a minute or two, breaking it up with a spoon as you go.
4. Before it starts to burn, gently pour in your two (well shaken) tins of coconut milk and mix in well. Then add your pint of chicken stock. Leave this on a medium heat, and then lower as needed if it starts to boil over.
5. Start your timer - set it for 20 minutes. Go!
6. Throw in your portions of white fish in to the soup, and make sure they're fully submerged. Adjust the temperature if necessary to keep it simmering.
7. At 10 minutes left on the timer, throw in your frozen gyoza. Give the fish a poke, it should be feeling most of the way cooked. We'll be overcooking it slightly to get the fishy goodness in to the soup. You'll want to keep stirring this gently, to make sure the gyoza don't make friends with the bottom of the pan.
8. Boil the kettle. At 6 minutes left on the timer, pour your freshly boiled water in to the bowl filled with the beans, peas, crunchy greens and baby sweetcorn. Cover with a plate to keep the temperature in.
9. At five minutes, chuck your noodles in to the smaller pan of boiling water.
10. Slice your red pepper in to fine rings. At 1 minute, drain your noodles and lightly break them up. Quickly pop them in the bottom of the bowls you'll be serving in.
11. At 0 minutes, take the soup off the heat and drain your blanched veg bowl.
12. Give the veg a good steamy jumble around to make sure you get most of the water off.
13. Portion out the fish and gyoza in to bowls (I find tongs good for this).
14. Pour the soup over the noodles, gyoza and fish.
15. Layer your blanched veg in a pretty pattern on top of the soup, hanging off the side of the bowl if you're feeling very artsy.
16. Garnish with the red pepper rings, and sprinkle with sesame seeds.
17. Serve with fork and spoon!

Serves 4

30 minutes

Recipe contributed from Milton Keynes, UK

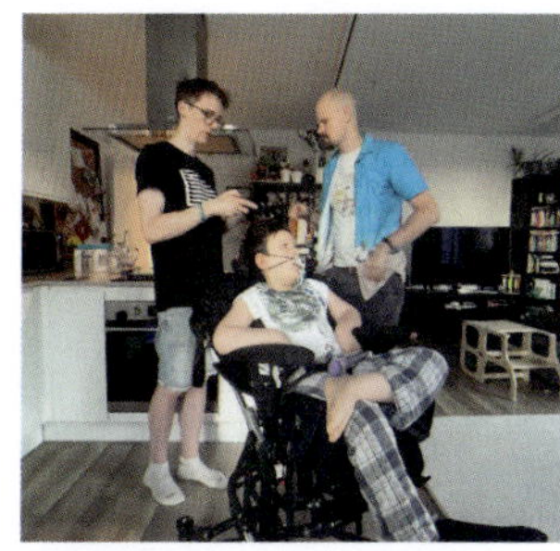

ABOUT

The exciting story with this recipe is very boring. I had a noodle soup round a friend's house that I really liked, and then rather than ask them for the recipe I spent months of trial and error trying to make something similar but with more punch. It's always a bit different but it's become a real staple.

Shared by Mike (and Laura!) Collins. We're pals with Sam, and Elly (and Mikaere + Tig!) Not sure what else to say! I've known Sam for multiple decades?

EASY SCOTTISH LENTIL
SOUP

DIRECTIONS

1. Finely chop the onion and leek and set aside, then chop the carrot, potato, and neep into small, bite sized pieces.
2. Heat the pot and add the butter or butter alternative. Add the onions and leek and cook for about 5 minutes. Don't let the onion brown.
3. Rinse the red lentils in cold water. Don't soak them.
4. Add the rest of the vegetables and cook for 1-2 minutes, then add the stock and lentils.
5. Bring to a boil then turn down to simmer for 40 minutes. You may need to top up with a little extra water if the soup gets too thick.
6. Serve with bannocks, crusty bread, or oatcakes.

NOTES

If you want to make the soup traditionally, you can add ham hock (also known as a pork knuckle)/gammon. If using Gammon that is heavily salted, you may want to soak it either overnight or for 2 hours before starting the recipe (UK gammon is typically mild, so perhaps might not be needed. Make sure you taste before adding any salt!)!

If you're using a ham hock/gammon then add to a pot with 1.5 litres of cold water, bring to boil and turn down to simmer for 2 hours. Remove the hock/gammon, set aside, and drain the stock into a jug. Continue with the recipe.

Once the soup is ready you can shred the hock/gammon and stir some back through the soup. If using smoked bacon, fry it up and throw it in at the end, and if you like, give it a short blitz with a stick blender.

Serves 6-8

60 minutes

Recipe contributed from New Zealand - Thanks Carrie Callaghan!

INGREDIENTS

1.5 cups red lentils

1 medium potato

1 small neep/swede

1 large carrot

1 leek

1 onion (about 200g)

1.5 litres of ham or veggie stock

30g/1oz butter

1 ham hock/gammon/smoked bacon

*optional

CHICKEN RICE
SOUP

Serves 2-3

90 minutes

Recipe contributed from New Zealand - Thanks Carrie Callaghan!

INGREDIENTS

1 tablespoon oil

1 onion minced

3 large carrots peeled and diced

1 stalk celery diced

1 teaspoon garlic minced

1 teaspoon fresh parsley

½ teaspoon dried thyme

1 teaspoon salt

⅛ teaspoon black pepper

5 cups low sodium chicken broth

2 chicken breasts uncooked

1 cup brown rice (do not use white rice)

1 cup evaporated milk

DIRECTIONS

1. In a large soup pot, heat oil over medium-high heat. Add onion, carrots and celery and cook and stir for 3-4 minutes, until onion begins to turn golden.
2. Add garlic, parsley (save some for the garnish) and thyme and cook 1 minute.
3. Add salt and pepper, broth, chicken. Add rice. Stir and bring to a boil over medium-high heat.
4. Reduce heat to medium-low (a simmer), cover, and cook for 30 minutes, stirring every 10 minutes, or until vegetables and rice are tender.
5. Remove chicken from pot and shred. Add back to the pot with evaporated milk.
6. Garnish with parsley and serve.

PUMPKIN + CHESTNUT
SOUP

DIRECTIONS

1. If you are using raw chestnuts, preheat the oven to fan 180°C/ 355 °F. Put each chestnut flat-side down on a chopping board. Using a sharp knife, cut a long slit on the top. Tip the nuts onto a roasting tin and arrange them cut-side up. Roast for 30 mins. The cuts should open up and the shell will start to peel back. Leave the nuts in the tin and put a board on top while they cool to trap the steam. This make them easier to peel. Once cool, peel the skin and remove the inner membrane too.
2. In the meantime, peel and chop pumpkin, onion and garlic.
3. Melt a knob of butter in a pan, add the onion, pumpkin and garlic. Cover and steam for 10 minutes.
4. Set some chestnuts aside for serving.
5. Add chestnuts, milk, salt, thyme, clove, cinnamon and cook for 30 minutes covered.
6. Blend and add nutmeg and pepper to taste.
7. Top with crushed chestnuts, flat leaf parsely and roasted pumpkin seeds and serve!

Serves 6-8

50 minutes

Recipe contributed from France

INGREDIENTS

800g pumpkin

400g chestnuts (pre-cooked or raw)

1 onion

1 garlic clove

1L milk

1 sprig of thyme

1 clove

2 pinches of cinnamon

Nutmeg

Salt and pepper

Flat leaf parsley and roasted pumpkin seeds, for garnish

ABOUT

Submited by Delphine, a wonderful friend of Elly + Sam's. This is her Mama's recipe, translated from French!

TORTILLA
SOUP

INGREDIENTS

2 dried Guajillo or ancho chiles

8 corn tortillas

2 14oz cans diced fire-roasted tomatoes

2 tablespoons avocado oil

1 large white onion

1½ teaspoon sea salt

1 teaspoon ground cumin

¼ teaspoon dried oregano

3 garlic cloves, grated

4 cups vegetable broth

3 cups cooked black beans

1½ cups frozen corn kernels

Freshly ground black pepper

For serving:

Diced avocado

Sliced radishes

Fresh cilantro

Crumbled Cotija cheese

Lime wedges

Serves 4-6

Recipe contributed from the UK

60 minutes

DIRECTIONS

1. Preheat the oven to 190°C/375°F and line two baking sheets with parchment paper.
2. Use scissors to slice the stems off the chililes, then cut open vertically along one edge. Spread open so they lay flat.
3. In a dry skillet over medium heat, toast the chiles for 1 to 2 minutes per side, or until soft and fragrant.
4. Place one of the tortillas in the pan and toast on each side until puffed up and fragrant.
5. Place the toasted chililes and tortilla in a blender and add the tomatoes. Blend until smooth.
6. Heat the avocado oil in a large pot over medium heat.
7. Add the onion and salt, and cook, stirring occasionally, for 8 minutes, or until softened.
8. Add the cumin and oregano and cook for 30 seconds, or until fragrant. Add the tomato mixture and cook, stirring, for 2 minutes. Add the garlic, water, and beans and simmer for 20 minutes. Add the corn and simmer for 10 more minutes.
9. Cut the remaining tortillas into thin strips and place on the prepared baking sheets. Drizzle with avocado oil, sprinkle with salt, and toss to coat. Spread evenly on the baking sheets and bake for 10 to 15 minutes, or until crispy.
10. If the soup is too thick, stir in a little more water to reach your desired consistency. Season to taste.
11. Ladle the soup into bowls and top with the crispy tortilla strips, reserved diced onion, avocado, radishes, cilantro, and Cotija cheese.
12. Serve with lime wedges for squeezing.

SWEETCORN MANGO
SALAD

DIRECTIONS

1. Remove the husks from the corn, and cook the cobs in just boiiling water for 10 minutes. Drain, and cut the kernels from the cob and add to your salad bowl.
2. Chop the red capsicum, avocado and mango in small, bite size cubes, about the size of your pinky nail, and add to the bowl.
3. Strip the leaves from the coriander, discard the stalks, and roughly chop. Add to the bowl.
4. Juice the lime and add to the bowl.
5. Mix well, and season to taste.

NOTES

This one is very easy. Use frozen corn, if sweetcorn isn't in season. You can also add red chilli, if you'd like!

Serves 3-4

20 minutes

Recipe contributed from Aoeteroa/New Zealand

INGREDIENTS

2-3 sweetcorn cobs

1 red pepper/capsicum

1 bunch of coriander/cilantro

1 avocado

1 mango

1 lime

AVOCADO CORN
SALAD

Serves 4-6

20 minutes

Recipe contributed from the UK

DIRECTIONS

1. Fill a large pot with enough water to cover the corn and bring to a boil. Shuck the corn and drop the corn into the boiling water. Cover and reduce heat to medium.
2. Cook corn until the kernels are tender, 6 to 8 minutes.
3. Quarter the tomatoes, thinly slice the red onion, mince the garlic, slice the avocado, finely chop the coriander and add to a bowl.
4. Once the corn is cooked, cut the kernels from the cob, and add to the bowl, with the spinach.
5. Drizzle the top with the extra virgin olive oil, lime juice, and season to taste.
6. Toss the salad gently just until combined and serve with a slice of lime.

INGREDIENTS

450g/1lb cherry tomatoes

2 tablespoons extra virgin olive oil

3 tablespoons fresh lime juice

2 garlic cloves

3 ears of corn

3 avocados

handful of spinach

½ medium red onion

½ small bunch of coriander/cilantro

'BRING SOMETHING' PASTA SALAD

DIRECTIONS

1. If your pine nuts aren't already toasted, bake in a single layer on a baking tray at 180 °C/350 °F for 5 to 7 minutes, until lightly brown and fragrant.
2. Bring a large pot of salted water to a boil. Prepare the pasta according to the package directions, or until slightly past al dente.
3. Meanwhile, make the dressing. In a small bowl, whisk together the olive oil, lemon juice, mustard, garlic, italian herbs, + salt.
4. Drain the pasta, toss it with a little olive oil (so that it doesn't stick together) and let it cool to room temp.
5. Transfer to a large bowl with the tomatoes, chickpeas, spinach, cucumbers, basil, parsley, mint, and pine nuts.
6. Pour the dressing and toss to coat. Season to taste with more lemon, salt, pepper, and/or a drizzle of olive oil, if desired.
7. Crumble the feta over the top, and serve.

Serves 4-6

35 minutes

Recipe contributed from the UK

INGREDIENTS

3 cups uncooked fusilli pasta

2 cups halved cherry tomatoes

1 ½ cups cooked chickpeas, drained and rinsed

2 cups spinach, chopped

1 cup cucumbers, sliced into thin quarters

1 cup crumbled feta cheese

1 cup torn basil leaves

½ cup minced parsley

½ cup finely chopped mint

¼ cup toasted pine nuts

¼ cup extra-virgin olive oil

3 tablespoons fresh lemon juice (approx 1.5 lemons)

½ teaspoon Dijon mustard

3 garlic cloves, minced

1 teaspoon dried Italian herbs

¼ teaspoon salt

NOTES

When you're going to a BBQ, or a potluck, this is the salad you bring. It's delicious, easy and perfect for gatherings!

STONE FRUIT CHICKEN
SALAD

DIRECTIONS

1. If you don't already have leftovers, cook your brown rice.
2. Rinse the rice in a fine mesh colander under running water to remove excess starch.
3. Bring a large pot of water to boil, using 6 cups water per 1 cup rice. Add the rice to the boiling water. Reduce the heat and maintain a steady boil. Boil, uncovered, for 30 minutes.
4. Drain off the remaining cooking water and return to pot.
5. Cover the pot and let the rice rest, off the heat, for 10 minutes.
6. Fluff, season as desired, and let cool.
7. Remove the chicken from the fridge 30 minutes before cooking to bring up to room temperature.
8. Preheat the oven to 180°C/369°F.
9. Generously season both sides of the chicken breasts.
10. Place a non-stick pan over a high heat, once smoking add a drizzle of olive oil and place the chicken breasts skin down.
11. Cook each side for about 5 minutes or until the chicken skin is golden and crisp.
12. Place in the oven and cook for 15–20 minutes. The flesh should be firm and white (not pink) and juices should run clear.
13. Rest the chicken for 5 minutes before chopping into chunks.
14. In the meantime, make the vinaigrette. Combine 2 tablespoons of olive oil, lemon zest, lemon juice, and mustard in a large bowl, stirring well with a whisk.
15. Add the chopped, cooked chicken, nectarines, rice, cherries, spring onions, torn mint and toss well, making sure the vinaigrette covers everything evenly.
16. Serve on a bed of rocket, and sprinkle with the chopped almonds.

Serves 4

45 minutes

Recipe contributed from the UK

INGREDIENTS

SALAD

3 (180g/6oz) skinless, boneless chicken breast halves

1 teaspoon salt, divided

½ teaspoon black pepper, divided

3 tablespoons torn mint

1 ½ cups coarsely chopped nectarines

1 cup cooked and cooled brown rice

1 cup coarsely chopped cherries

½ cup sliced spring onions/scallions

¼ cup dry-roasted almonds, chopped

1 fistful of rocket/arugula per serving.

VINAIGRETTE

2 tablespoons olive oil

1 teaspoon lemon zest

2 tablespoons fresh lemon juice

½ teaspoon dijon mustard

KALE AND GINGER CARROT
SALAD

DIRECTIONS

1. Preheat the oven to 220°C/425°F and line a large baking sheet with parchment paper.
2. Spread the chickpeas on a kitchen towel and pat them dry.
3. Remove any loose skins.
4. Transfer the dried chickpeas to the baking sheet and toss them with a drizzle of olive oil and generous pinches of salt.
5. Chop all but the smallest of the raw carrots, clear a section of the tray and add the carrots.
6. Roast the chickpeas until golden brown and crispy and the carrots are soft (around 20-30 minutes).
7. Transfer the carrots to a blender and add the water, olive oil, rice vinegar, ginger, and salt. Blend the dressing until smooth and chill in the fridge.
8. Wash and dry the kale leaves and place into a large bowl and drizzle with the lemon juice, ½ teaspoon of olive oil, and a few pinches of salt.
9. Massage the leaves until they become soft and wilted and reduce in the bowl by about half.
10. Grate the reserved small carrot, and the beet, thinly slice the watermelon radish and add to the bowl.
11. Cube the avocado, and add half to the bowl, with cranberries, pepitas, a few more good pinches of salt and a few grinds of pepper, and toss.
12. Drizzle generously with the carrot ginger dressing. Top with the remaining avocado, more dressing, the roasted chickpeas and sprinkle with the sesame seeds.
13. Season to taste and serve.

Serves 4

45 minutes

Recipe contributed from the UK

INGREDIENTS

1 ½ cups cooked chickpeas, drained and rinsed

4-5 carrots

½ cup water

¼ cup extra-virgin olive oil

2 tablespoons rice vinegar

2 teaspoons minced ginger

¼ teaspoon sea salt

1 bunch curly kale, stems removed, leaves torn

1 teaspoon lemon juice

½ teaspoon extra-virgin olive oil

1 small red beet

½ watermelon radish,

1 avocado

2 tablespoons dried cranberries

¼ cup toasted pumpkin seeds/pepitas

1 teaspoon sesame seeds

GREEK
SALAD

Serves 4

Recipe contributed from the UK

15 minutes

INGREDIENTS

SALAD

1 cucumber

1 green bell pepper/capsicum

2 cups cherry tomatoes

150g/5oz feta cheese

½ red onion

⅓ cup pitted Kalamata olives

⅓ cup fresh mint leaves

DRESSING

¼ cup extra-virgin olive oil

3 tablespoons red wine vinegar

1 garlic clove, minced

½ teaspoon dried oregano

¼ teaspoon dijon mustard

¼ teaspoon sea salt

Freshly ground black pepper

DIRECTIONS

1. Cut the cucumber lengthwise and slice ½ -cm/¼-inch thick.
2. Chop the green bell pepper into thumb size pieces, and halve the cherry tomatoes. and thinly slice the red onion.
3. Cut the feta into ½ inch cubes.
4. On a large platter, arrange the cucumber, green pepper, cherry tomatoes, feta cheese, red onions, and olives.
5. Make the dressing: In a small bowl, whisk together the olive oil, vinegar, garlic, oregano, mustard, salt, and several grinds of pepper.
6. Drizzle the salad with the dressing and very gently toss.
7. Sprinkle with a few generous pinches of oregano and top with the mint leaves.
8. Season to taste and serve.

WATERMELON AND FETA
SALAD

DIRECTIONS

1. Chop 180g watermelon and ½ cucumber into chunks and tip into a bowl with most of the leaves from ½ bunch of mint.
2. Drizzle with 1 tbsp olive oil.
3. Season and pile on to a serving plate.
4. Crumble over 100g feta, the remaining mint leaves, then drizzle with 1 tbsp balsamic glaze just before serving.

NOTES

Balsamic glaze is a reduction of balsamic vinegar, and is very delicious! You can also add rocket, or very finely chopped red chilli for a bit of a kick.

Serves 4

15 minutes

Recipe contributed from the UK

INGREDIENTS

180g/6.5oz watermelon

½ cucumber

½ bunch mint

1 tablespoon olive oil

100g/3.5oz feta

1 tablespoon balsamic glaze

BEETROOT + HALLOUMI
SALAD

DIRECTIONS

1. Preheat the oven to 200°C/400°F, and on a tray drizzle beetroot with olive oil and salt, and bake for 40 to 45 minutes or until the beets are soft but not shrunken.
2. On a separate tray, add the walnuts for the last 5 - 7 minutes.
3. Allow both beets + walnuts to cool slightly.
4. Peel the beetroot (wear gloves), and chop into cubes.
5. Roughly chop the walnuts.
6. Combine the chopped parsley, lemon juice, olive oil and minced garlic in a bowl, and whisk.
7. Slice the halloumi into ½cm/¼in thick slices. Heat a dry frying pan over a medium heat, and toast for 2–3 minutes on both sides, or until the halloumi is golden-brown.
8. In a bowl, add the beetroot, and halloumi, toss in the lemon vingaigrette and season with salt and black pepper to taste.
9. Garnish with the chopped walnut and serve.

Serves 4

60 minutes

Recipe contributed from the UK

INGREDIENTS

4 medium beetroots

250g/8.5oz halloumi cheese

90g/3oz walnuts

2 tablespoons chopped parsley

3 tablespoons lemon juice

3 tablespoons olive oil

4 minced garlic cloves

THAI PORK LARB GAI
SALAD

DIRECTIONS

1. Cook the mince in a non-stick skillet with no oil. Cook thoroughly and keep the juices in the pan.
2. Once the pork is cooked, remove from heat and stir in sliced red onions, which should wilt slightly.
3. Add the toasted rice powder, lime juice, fish sauce, and Thai chilli flakes.
4. Taste, and add more lime, fish sauce, or chilli as needed.
5. Top with the whole mint leaves and coriander.
6. Serve with sliced lettuce and/or a side of rice.

NOTES

You can use substitute any kind of ground mince, turkey, chicken or beef. Toasted rice powder can be bought from any Asian supermarket, but you can also make it at home. 2 tablespoons of uncooked, sweet sticky rice grains to a pan over medium heat. Toast until the grains have some colour and become fragrant. Place in a spice grinder or blender and blend until very fine. If using a blender, pour the rice mix through a strainer to remove any large pieces, as you want to end up with a fine powder.

Serves 4

25 minutes

Recipe contributed from the UK

INGREDIENTS

450g/1lb pork mince

½ cup thinly sliced red onion

1 tablespoon toasted rice powder

1-2 tablespoons fish sauce

2-3 tablespoons fresh lime juice

1 tablespoon ground Thai chilli peppers

⅓ cup coriander/cilantro leaves

¼ cup whole mint leaves

THE BITESIZE
SALAD

Serves 4

Recipe contributed from the UK

15 minutes

INGREDIENTS

2 baby gem lettuce

1 fistful of spinach

2-3 sprigs basil

2-3 sprigs mint

1 mini pot of salad cress

1 avocado

1 celery stem

1 red bell pepper/capsicum

½ cucumber

200g sugarsnap peas

15-20 cherry tomatoes

15-20 grapes or **1-2** kiwifruit

⅔ cup olive oil

⅓ cup fresh lemon juice

DIRECTIONS

1. Slice baby gem lettuce across into ribbons. Strip the leaves from the basil and mint, discard the stalks, and roughly chop, along with the spinach. Snip the top of the cress from the roots. Add all of the above to a salad bowl.
2. Chop everything else into small, 1cm bite size pieces, ensuring everything is similarly sized and add to salad.
3. Make the vinaigrette: whisk oil and lemon juice in a small bowl or shake in a resealable jar to emulsify; season with salt and pepper.
4. Add vinaigrette to salad, toss to combine and serve.

PEA AND BACON SUMMER
SALAD

Serves 4

Recipe contributed from the US

45 minutes

INGREDIENTS

4 cups frozen peas, thawed

½ cup shredded sharp cheddar cheese

½ cup ranch salad dressing

⅓ cup chopped red onion

4 bacon strips, cooked and crumbled

DIRECTIONS

1. First, combine the peas, cheese, ranch salad dressing and red onion and toss to coat.
2. Refrigerate, covered, at least 30 minutes.
3. In the meantime, fry the bacon until very crisp, and crumble.
4. Stir in the crumbled bacon just before serving.

THE WHATEVER QUINOA
SALAD

INGREDIENTS

2 cups quinoa

½ jar sundried tomatoes, drained

200g mozzarella cheese pearls

200g cooked chicken pieces

1 green bell pepper/capsicum

Serves 4-6

30 minutes

Recipe contributed from the UK

Anything else you have on hand, or fancy in the deli aisle: Olives, artichokes, fallafel, peas, cucumber, nuts, sultanas or dried apricots, feta, chickpeas, leftover bean salad, cherry tomatoes, avocado, red onion, fresh basil or coriander/cilantro, spinach or kale, courgette or roast sweet potato, smoked hummus etc.

DIRECTIONS

1. Rinse the quinoa in cold water, then, in a pot, add two and a half cups of boiling water. Bring to a boil, cover and reduce the heat, simmer for 15 minutes.
2. Remove from the heat, and let it sit (covered) for another 10 minutes.
3. Remove cover, allow to cool, and fluff with a fork.
4. Chop the sundried tomatoes, chicken and bell pepper into bite sized pieces, along with whatever else you're adding.
5. Mix into the quinoa, with the mozzerella pearls.
6. Season with salt and pepper, and drizzle with a vinaigrette if you fancy (very optional).

NOTES

Super versatile and good for using up all the leftover things! Don't skip washing the quinoa, you need to remove the saponins which are very bitter. The trick with this salad is to make sure everything is bite sized and to balance the textures: you want a mix of crunchy and soft. Super delicious, and a fun reason to cruise the deli aisle!

BROCCOLI AND ALMOND
SALAD

Serves 4

Recipe contributed from the UK

15 minutes

INGREDIENTS

450g/1lb broccoli crowns

3 tablespoons extra-virgin olive oil

3 tablespoons good quality mayo

1½ tablespoons apple cider vinegar

1 teaspoon Dijon mustard

1 teaspoon maple syrup or honey

1 garlic clove, minced

¼ teaspoon sea salt, more to taste

⅓ cup diced red onions

⅓ cup dried cranberries

½ cup almonds

½ cup pumpkin seeds/pepitas

1 tablespoon tamari

½ teaspoon maple syrup

¼ teaspoon smoked paprika

DIRECTIONS

1. Preheat the oven to 180°C/350°F and line a baking sheet with parchment paper.
2. Chop the broccoli florets into ½-inch pieces and any remaining stems into ¼-inch dice. (Because the broccoli is raw, it's important to cut small enough to become fully coated and soften in the dressing).
3. In a large bowl, whisk together the olive oil, mayo, apple cider vinegar, mustard, maple syrup, garlic, and salt. Add the broccoli, onions, and cranberries and toss to coat.
4. Place the almonds and pumpkin seeds on the baking sheet, toss with the tamari, maple syrup, and smoked paprika and spread into a thin layer.
5. Bake 10 to 14 minutes or until golden brown. Remove from the oven and let cool for 5 minutes (they'll get crispier as they sit).
6. Toss the almonds and pumpkin seeds into the salad, reserving a few to sprinkle on top. Season to taste and serve.

PANZANELLA
SALAD

DIRECTIONS

1. Preheat oven to 180°C/ 350°F
2. Chop tomatoes into bite sized pieces. Place in a colander set over a bowl and season with 2 teaspoons kosher salt. Toss to coat. Set aside at room temperature to drain, tossing occasionally. Drain for a minimum of 15 minutes.
3. Cut bread into 1 ½ inch cubes and in a large bowl, toss with 2 tablespoons of olive oil and transfer to a baking sheet.
4. Bake about 15 minutes, until crisp and firm but not browned. Remove from oven and let cool.
5. Remove the colander with tomatoes to the sink. In the tomato juice bowl, add the minced glaric, minced spring onion, mustard and vinegar.
6. Whisking constantly, drizzle in remaining (120ml) olive oil.
7. Season dressing to taste with salt and pepper.
8. Combine toasted bread, tomatoes, and dressing in a large bowl. Add basil leaves.
9. Toss everything to coat and season with salt and pepper. Let rest 30 minutes before serving, tossing occasionally until the dressing is absorbed by the bread.
10. Add the torn mozzarella on top and serve.

Serves 4-6

30 minutes

Recipe contributed from the UK

INGREDIENTS

1kg/2lb mixed ripe tomatoes,

3 tablespoons kosher salt

340g/¾lb ciabatta/sourdough bread

150ml extra-virgin olive oil

2 tablespoons minced spring onion/shallot

2 medium cloves garlic, minced

½ teaspoon Dijon mustard

2 tablespoons white wine vinegar or red wine vinegar

Freshly ground black pepper

½ cup packed basil leaves, roughly chopped

250g mozzarella, drained and torn

MAINS

CREAMY PRAWN PASTA

MAIN

DIRECTIONS

1. Bring to boil a large pot of water. Add pasta and cook per packet MINUS 1 minute.
2. Just before draining, scoop out 1 cup of pasta cooking water and set aside. Drain pasta.
3. Meanwhile, melt butter in a large pot over medium high heat. Once melted, add garlic. Stir for 20 seconds until fragrant.
4. Add white wine and stir. Simmer for 2 minutes until wine mostly reduces.
5. Add cream, broth and parmesan. Stir until the parmesan is melted, then leave to simmer for 1-2 minutes.
6. Add prawns, stir, then add pasta.
7. Toss the pasta while still on the heat. Add a small amount of the reserved pasta water, and the sauce will thicken in about 30 - 45 seconds and start clinging to the pasta.
8. Move it off the heat just before the sauce is as thick as you like it - as it will thicken more.
9. Season with pepper (and salt, though taste test to see if you need it) and toss the pasta again.
10. Add a tiny splash of pasta water if the sauce is too thick.
11. Plate, garnish with chopped parsley and more parmesan.

Serves 4

25 minutes

Recipe contributed from the UK

INGREDIENTS

250g/8oz fresh tagliatelle

30g/1oz butter

300g/10oz precooked prawns

3 garlic cloves, minced

65ml/¼ cup dry white wine

250ml/1 cup double/heavy cream

125ml/½ cup chicken broth

50g/1.5oz freshly, finely grated parmesan cheese

2 tablespoons chopped parsley

Black pepper

Extra finely grated parmesan cheese

NOTES

You can use any dry white (such as a sauvignon or a white rioja - avoid very fruity whites). If you'd prefer, you can substitute with chicken or veg broth. Use full fat cream, this is not the recipe for counting calories. Using light/skim will affect the consistency of the sauce. Make sure you use freshly grated parmesan - store-bought won't melt in the same way and might be bitty. You can also add cherry tomatoes or peas if you want to add some freshness!

MERCY'S FRESH FISH

MAIN

DIRECTIONS

1. In a blender, add the tomatoes, uziza seed, ground calabash, negro peppers, sweet pepper, stock cubes, fresh ginger + the garlic cloves.
2. Whizz until it's a smooth paste (you may need to add a small amount of water, but take note of how much water you add).
3. Add your paste, and 900ml of water (enough to turn the two stock cubes into stock, minus the amount you already added in the paste) and simmer for 45-60 minutes or so.
4. Add the fish, and simmer until the fish is cooked through.
5. Add the scent leaves/uzazi for five minutes to brew before serving.

Serves 4

90 minutes

Recipe contributed from the UK

INGREDIENTS

500g fish of choice (we like it with white fish!)

2 tablespoons uziza seed

2 teaspoons ground Calabash nutmeg

2 fresh tomatoes

6 whole black Negro peppers

1 sweet pepper

2 stock cubes (fish, chicken or vegetable)

2-3 Scent leaves or Uzazi leaves

40g fresh ginger

20g/3 garlic cloves

ABOUT

This recipe was submitted by Mercy, one of Mikaere's nurses. She's been taking care of Mikaere for almost half his life, and we're so grateful for her!

HELEN'S FISH PIE

MAIN

Serves 4

Recipe contributed from Aotearoa/New Zealand

40 minutes

INGREDIENTS

Any kind of fish or seafood, raw

½ cup of flour

¼ cup of butter

2 cups of milk

2 sheets of flaky puff pastry

DIRECTIONS

1. Strip fish off bones.
2. Make white sauce, adding a bit of flour at a time to warm milk in a pot, constantly stirring until smooth.
3. Add fish to sauce.
4. Line pie dish with pastry, and add fish and sauce.
5. Add the pastry lid.
6. Back at 180 °C/350 °F for 20-30 minutes, until pastry is cooked and golden brown.

ABOUT

This recipe was submitted by Liz, Elly's best friend. Helen (Liz's Mama) was such a beautiful person. Elly was always, always welcome in their home. Helen is so loved, and sorely missed.

ELLY'S FISH PIE

MAIN

DIRECTIONS

1. Heat the oven fan 180 °C/350 °F.
2 Put the potatoes, peeled and halved, in a saucepan and pour over enough water to cover them. Bring to a boil and then simmer until tender.
3. Chop the carrots, courgettes and broccoli into bite-sized pieces and set aside.
4. When the potatoes are cooked, drain thoroughly and mash with a splash of milk and a knob of butter. Season with ground black pepper.
5. In a new pot, put the butter and plain flour on a medium-high heat, stirring until it's combined together, around 1-2 minutes.
6. Gradually whisk in the milk on the heat, stirring constantly to avoid any lumps and sticking at the bottom of the pan. It should take 3-4 minutes to thicken.
7. Take off the heat and stir in the fish, the frozen peas, the carrots, courgette and broccoli. Spoon into an ovenproof dish.
8. Spoon the potato on top.
9. Pop in the oven for 20-25 mins or until golden and bubbling at the edges. Allow to cool slightly before serving.

Serves 4-6

45 minutes

Recipe contributed from the UK

INGREDIENTS

750g/27oz mixed fish and seafood (salmon, cod, haddock, hake, prawns, mussels), raw, skinned and deboned.

1 cup frozen peas

2 Carrots

2 courgettes/zucchini

½ broccoli head

1kg/2lb potatoes (like Maris Piper) peeled and halved

400ml milk, plus a splash

40g butter, plus a knob

40g plain flour

CRAB BAKE

MAIN

DIRECTIONS

1. Whizz up your bread, cheese and parsley in a food processor until nicely chopped. You might need to do this in batches.
2. Put in a large bowl.
3. Fold in the crab meat with a few drops of Worcestershire sauce and then add as much cream (or milk) required to make a soft mix.
4. Grease a shallow ovenproof dish with butter and then add your bake. Fork the top up slightly.
5. Bake at 180 °C/350 °F or hotter for about 20 mins until the top is golden brown.
6. Serve with vegetables and a squeeze of lemon.

NOTES

This can also be made with tuna or salmon and is lovely with whichever fish you choose. Ingredients are very easy to scale up or down to suit!

ABOUT

This recipe was submitted by Wendy, Mikaere's Grandma, Sam's Mum. She says: I loved this recipe (adapted from a very old recipe book by Zena Skinner. She used to be on TV in the 70s!) when my children were small because you can make it in moments and put it in the fridge until required! Ideal to make in the morning when you have a bit more energy... I still love it now when I don't have much time or ingredients.

Serves 2-4

30 minutes

Recipe contributed from the UK

INGREDIENTS

145g crab (either canned or fresh)

3-4 slices of bread - white or brown

As much cheddar cheese as you like

Parsley (optional)

Worcestershire sauce, dried paprika, or chilli sauce.

Cream/milk

Butter for dish greasing

SAM'S PRAWN COUS COUS

MAIN

DIRECTIONS

1. Place a large pan or wok on medium heat with some olive oil, slice up the peppers and toss in the pan to heat for about 5 minutes until the edges are beginning to brown.
2. Mince the garlic and add until fragrant. Add in the couscous and mixed Italian herbs then quickly mix so the couscous is coated in olive oil. Take off the heat if required to prevent the couscous from toasting too much.
3. Add chicken stock and canned tomatoes and stir in.
4. Season and then cover the pan and let it simmer gently for 6 - 10 minutes. Stir periodically.
5. In the meantime, cut the lemon into wedges for serving and set aside. Add zest and juice from the remaining lemon to the pan and stir. Chop a handful of fresh basil and parsley.
6. After most of the liquid has been absorbed, stir in the prawns, fresh basil and half the parsley. Cook for another 5 - 8 minutes so the prawns warm through.
7. Garnish with the lemon wedges and remaining parsley and voila! Serve!

Serves 2-4

30 minutes

Recipe contributed from the UK

INGREDIENTS

2 peppers/capsicum (red + green)

300g giant couscous

300g precooked king prawns

1 ½ teaspoon mixed Italian herbs

2 garlic cloves

250ml chicken stock

1 can chopped tomatoes

1 lemon

fresh basil + parsley

SIMPLE COD + PARMA HAM

MAIN

Serves 4

Recipe contributed from Leicestershire, UK

30 minutes

INGREDIENTS

4 cod steaks, skinless (or other firm white fish such as haddock or hake)

4 90g packets of Parma ham

4 head of broccoli (or other green veg of your choice)

4 250g packet cooked lentils, flavour of your choice

Ground black pepper

Mayonnaise to serve

DIRECTIONS

1. Lay out 2 or 3 slices of the Parma ham (depending on the size of your fish steaks), side by side but overlapping slightly. Grind some black pepper over the top.
2. Lay one fish steak on top of the Parma ham slices, and fold the ham over it to make a simple parcel. Repeat with the other 3 fish steaks. Note: The fish steaks should not need any salt on them due to the saltiness of the Parma ham.
3. Heat a non-stick frying pan over a medium heat. Add the fish steak parcels to the pan (no oil should be necessary). Cook for 10 minutes, turning after 5 minutes. Check the fish steaks are cooked through.
4. Meanwhile cut the broccoli into florets and boil or steam for up to 10 minutes until cooked.
5. Heat the lentils as per the packet instructions, either in a microwave or in a pan on the hob.
6. Serve the fish steaks on heated plates, with the broccoli and a serving of lentils, and with the mayonnaise on the side.

ABOUT

Recipe submitted by David Highton - For several years I have joined Elly and her family on a Māori language journey, which has been a great source of friendship, fun and enlightenment.

(Ngā mihi nui e David! <3)

TERIYAKI SALMON + KALE

MAIN

DIRECTIONS

1. If making teriyaki sauce from scratch, add all ingredients to a small bowl, and stir until combined.
2 In a small baking dish, place the garlic and ginger with the salmon on top, skin side up. Cover with teriyaki sauce, and marinate in the fridge for at least an hour, ideally longer.
3. Preheat the oven to 200 °C/400 °F
4. Remove the salmon from the marinade, reserving the sauce, and place salmon skin side down on a parchment-lined baking tray.
5. Bake for 10-15 minutes, or until the salmon begins to flake.
6. Move the pan to the top rack to broil until the top of the salmon starts to colour, about 1-3 minutes - watch closely.
7. To prepare the glaze, simmer the reserved marinade in a saucepan over medium heat until thickened, about 10 minutes.
8. To prepare the kale, set a frying pan over medium heat. Add the oil, garlic and ginger, and cook until fragrant, about 1-2 minutes.
9. Add the kale, season with salt and pepper, then cover with a lid and cook for 3-5 minutes, until the kale is wilted but still a vibrant green.
10. Serve the salmon with the skin side down, and kale on the side. Brush the top of the fish with the glaze and garnish with sliced spring onion and sesame seeds.

Serves 2

90 minutes

Recipe contributed from the USA

INGREDIENTS

SALMON

½ cup teriyaki sauce (store bought or homemade)

2.5cm/1 inch piece of ginger, peeled and sliced

2 garlic cloves, crushed

180g/6oz salmon fillets

1 spring/green onion, finely sliced

1 teaspoon toasted sesame seeds

KALE

1 tablespoon olive oil

1 garlic clove, sliced

1.5cm/ ½ inch piece of ginger, peeled and sliced

3 cups roughly chopped kale

TERIYAKI SAUCE

½ cup hoisin sauce

¼ cup honey

¼ cup soy sauce

4 garlic cloves, minced

2.5cm/1 inch piece of ginger, grated

1 tablespoon sesame oil

CULLEN SKINK

MAIN

Serves 4

Recipe contributed from Scotland

40 minutes

INGREDIENTS

1 tablespoon unsalted butter

1 medium onion

400g medium potatoes (about 2), peeled and cut into 1cm cubes

250g smoked haddock

250ml whole milk

½ small bunch of parsley or chives, finely chopped

DIRECTIONS

1. Melt the butter in a saucepan over a medium heat, then add the onion and fry for 5-8 mins until translucent but not browned.
2. Add the potatoes and 300ml water and bring to the boil.
3. Reduce the heat slightly and simmer for 10-15 mins.
4. Meanwhile, put the haddock in another pan and cover with the milk. Cook gently for 5 mins, or until just tender.
5. Remove the haddock from the milk with a slotted spoon (reserving the milk), transfer to a plate and leave to cool slightly. When cool enough to touch, flake into large pieces, removing any bones.
6. Put the reserved milk and flaked haddock in the pan with the potato mixture and cook for another 5 minutes.
7. Season and sprinkle over the parsley to serve.

NOTES

This is a very Scottish soup. Typically an authentic Cullen skink will use finnan haddie (a type of cold-smoked haddock), but it can be made with any other undyed smoked haddock. This soup is a local speciality, from the town of Cullen in Moray, on the northeast coast of Scotland.

SOUTHWESTERN CHICKEN BREAD BOATS

MAIN

Serves 2

Recipe contributed from the USA

45 minutes

DIRECTIONS

1. Preheat the oven to 200 °C/400 °F.
2. Line a baking pan with foil and lightly grease with cooking spray; set aside.
3. Using a serrated knife, cut a wedge into the top of each loaf, cutting to about 1 inch from each side.
4. Using your fingers, carefully remove the cut wedge inside of each loaf.
5. Transfer bread boats to prepared baking pan, spray the inside of the boats with cooking spray and bake for 5 to 7 minutes, or until lightly crusted inside. (Do not skip, it prevents the awful soggy bottom, which is significantly less delicious).
6. Remove from oven and set aside.
7. Heat olive oil in a large nonstick skillet; add onions and cook for 2 minutes or until tender.
8. Add garlic and continue to cook until fragrant, 30 seconds.
9. Stir in the diced tomatoes; season with chili powder, cumin, paprika, salt and pepper.
10. Bring to a boil; reduce heat to a simmer and continue to cook for 5 minutes, stirring occasionally.
11. Stir in chicken, corn, and black beans til just warm (3 minutes).
12. Spoon chicken mixture into prepared bread boats and top with cheese.
13. Bake for 10-12 minutes, until cheese has melted.
14. Remove from oven and let stand few minutes.
15. Dollop with light sour cream and sprinkle with chopped parsley or coriander/cilantro.

INGREDIENTS

1 12-14in loaf French Bread, cut into three equal pieces

2 tablespoons olive oil

1 yellow onion, diced

3 garlic cloves, minced

1 14.5oz can diced tomatoes

1/2 tablespoon chilli powder

1 teaspoon ground cumin

½ teaspoon paprika

2 cups cooked chicken, diced

½ cup frozen corn kernels

14.5oz/2 cups cooked black beans

1½ cups shredded cheese

fresh chopped parsley or cilantro

sour cream, for serving

NOTES

Some would say this is meant to be an appetiser or even a side. But those people are ridiculous, so don't listen.

CHICKEN GOULASH

MAIN

DIRECTIONS

1. In a large, heavy pot, heat the oil over moderately high heat.
2. Season the chicken with ¼ teaspoon of salt and add to the pan.
3. Cook the chicken until browned, turning, about 8 minutes in all. Remove. Pour off all but 1 tablespoon fat from the pan.
4. Add the onion, carrots, celery, and garlic to the pan. Reduce the heat to moderate and cook, stirring occasionally, until the onion is translucent, about 5 minutes.
5. Reduce the heat to moderately low and add the paprika, flour, and cayenne to the pan. Cook, stirring, for 30 seconds. Stir in the broth, tomatoes, the remaining 1 ¼ teaspoons salt, thyme, and the bay leaf. Add the chicken and bring to a simmer.
7. Reduce the heat and simmer, partially covered, until the chicken is done, about 20 minutes.
8. Remove the bay leaf and add the parsley and black pepper.
9. Serve! Wonderful with rice and a green salad.

Serves 2

90 minutes

Recipe contributed from Denmark

INGREDIENTS

1 tablespoon cooking oil

8 chicken thighs

1 ½ teaspoon salt

1 onion, chopped

2 carrots, cut into 1/4-inch slices

2 ribs celery, cut into 1/4-inch slices

2 cloves garlic, minced

2 tablespoons paprika

1 tablespoon flour

⅛ teaspoon cayenne

1 ½ cups canned low-sodium chicken broth or homemade stock

1 ½ cups canned crushed tomatoes in thick puree

¼ teaspoon dried thyme

1 bay leaf

ABOUT

Recipe submitted by the wonderful Claire Gudex, a friend of Elly and David Highton, who are all learning Te Reo Māori together. This recipe was her Mother's, Anne Gudex.

CREAMY LEMON CHICKEN WITH SPINACH AND ARTICHOKE

MAIN

Serves 4

Recipe contributed from the USA

35 minutes

INGREDIENTS

450g/1lb chicken cutlets

All-purpose flour, for dredging

2 tablespoons unsalted butter

2 tablespoons extra-virgin olive oil

3 garlic cloves, minced garlic

1 tablespoon fresh thyme leaves

1¼ cups chicken broth

110g/4oz cream cheese, room temperature

300g/10oz baby spinach

250g/9oz artichoke hearts, quartered

100g/3.5oz sundried tomatoes, chopped

3 tablespoons fresh lemon juice

30g/1oz finely grated parmesan

DIRECTIONS

1. Heat a large cast-iron skillet over medium-high.
2. Add butter and 1 tablespoon oil to skillet.

   Season chicken with salt and pepper; dredge in flour, shaking off any excess.
3. When butter melts, add chicken in a single layer and cook, flipping once, until golden brown in places but not cooked through, about 3 minutes. Transfer to a plate.
4. Add remaining 1 tablespoon oil, garlic, and thyme to skillet; cook until fragrant, 10 seconds. Stir in broth and cream cheese; cook until mixture boils and cheese melts.
5. Add spinach and cook, stirring, until wilted, 2 to 3 minutes. Stir in artichokes and sundried tomatoes; cook 1 minute more.
6. Return chicken and any juices to skillet. Simmer, shaking pan occasionally, until sauce is reduced and thickened slightly and chicken is just cooked through, about 3 minutes. Remove from heat; stir in lemon juice and cheese.
7. Serve over rice.

NOTES

We love artichoke dip, so this works well for us! It's also pretty flexible (for a visitor that didn't like artichokes, I used cherry tomatoes and capers instead). I've also thrown in a handful of prawns that I had on hand, and it was DELICIOUS! For those that like spice, you can add a sprinkle of heat from red pepper flakes.

THAI GREEN CHICKEN CURRY

MAIN

DIRECTIONS

1. Heat a large pan/wok over medium heat, add a dash of oil.
2. Add curry paste, garlic, and ginger and mix to get fragrant.
3. Add stock and coconut milk, and mix to dissolve the paste.
4. Add 1 teaspoon of fish sauce and 1 teaspoon of sugar. No need for salt as the fish sauce is salty enough.
5. Add lime leaves. Mix, then bring to a simmer.
6. Add the aubergine, cook for 4 minutes til they start to soften.
7. Add chicken and red pepper, stir then lower heat to medium so it's bubbling gently. Cook for 10 minutes.
8. Taste sauce. If needed, add half a teaspoon of fish sauce for more saltiness, or half a teaspoon of sugar for sweetness, til it's to your satisfaction.
9. Add the mangetout, cook for around 2 minutes until softened.
10. When the chicken is done, take off the heat and stir through basil and lime juice from one lime. Sauce should have reduced but will still be thin, not thick which is how it's meant to be.
11. Serve curry over rice with a wedge of lime.

Serves 2

45 minutes

Recipe contributed from the UK

INGREDIENTS

250ml/1 cup chicken stock

1 can of coconut milk

1 - 3 teaspoon fish sauce, to taste

1 - 3 teaspoon white sugar, to taste

3 tablespoons Thai green curry paste

400g chicken thigh (skinless/boneless)

1 small aubergine, thinly sliced

6 kaffir lime leaves

1 red pepper, thinly sliced

2 limes

2 garlic cloves, minced

1 thumb of ginger, grated

Mangetout, trimmed

Thai basil

NOTES

Use full fat, creamy coconut milk, we get ours from our local Asian supermarket. The lime leaves really provide a lot of flavour, don't skip these.

STIR FRIED CHICKEN WITH LIME AND COCONUT

MAIN

Serves 4

Recipe contributed from New Zealand

60 minutes for the marinade
35 minutes to cook

INGREDIENTS

2 boneless, skinless chicken breasts

1 cup jasmine rice

150ml tin of coconut milk

1 dessert spoon Thai fish sauce

4 heaped tablespoons fresh chopped coriander leaves

handful of green beans

1 dessert spoon olive oil

1 red chilli, deseeded and finely chopped

4 spring onions, finely chopped

Zest and juice from 1 large lime

DIRECTIONS

1. Chop the chicken into bite-sized pieces and place in a bowl with the lime juice and zest.
2. Stir well and leave to marinate for at least an hour. Rinse the rice to remove starch.
3. Bring 2¼ cups of water to a boil in a medium saucepan. Stir in the rice and ¾ teaspoon salt; cover the pan and reduce the heat to low.
4. Simmer for 15 minutes until all of the water is absorbed. Taste the rice to test for doneness; it should be perfectly cooked, but if it is still too firm, add a few more tablespoons of water, cover the pan, and let the rice absorb the water off the heat for a few more minutes.
5. While the rice is cooking, heat the oil in the pan or wok over high heat, add the chicken pieces and stir-fry for 3-4 minutes until they're golden.
6. Add the chilli, and chopped green beans, stir-fry for 1 more minute, and add the coconut milk, fish sauce and half the coriander and spring onions. Cook for another 1-2 minutes.
7. Serve the chicken over the rice and garnish with the remaining coriander and spring onions.

SUPER EASY CHICKEN PIE

MAIN

DIRECTIONS

1. Preheat the oven to fan 180 °C/350 °F.
2. If you don't have cooked chicken, or carrots now is the time. Roughly chop the carrots into largeish pieces and place into an oven-safe tray. Lay the chicken over the top, add a good splash of olive oil, salt and pepper and fan bake until the carrot is cooked but firm and the chicken is cooked all the way through (15/20 minutes, depending on size). Once cooked, strip the meat from the bones and shred, and chop the carrots into bitesize pieces.
3. In a large pot over medium heat, make the roux. Heat the butter, and once melted, add the flour. Stir until the butter is all soaked up, Very slowly, alternate adding (a little at a time) the milk, and then the stock, stirring until fully incorporated before adding more. It should be a thick, but smooth gravy.
4. Remove from heat and throw in the cooked, shredded chicken, carrots and peas. Chop the courgette into bite-size pieces, and add to the gravy. Season with salt and pepper and mix well.
5. Grease your pie dish with butter, and line with a piece of puff pastry. Add your filling, and then top with the second puff pastry piece, making sure the edges are sealed. Make three holes in the top so steam can escape.
6. Fan bake at 180 °C/350 °F for 30 minutes, or until the pastry is cooked through and golden.
7. Allow to stand for 10 minutes before serving.

NOTES

This pie is so forgiving, and well delicious. You can throw in any leftover vege you have: broccoli/cauliflower, mushrooms, spinach, sweetcorn etc. Can also be made in muffin tins, for mini pies!

Serves 4

30-50 minutes

Recipe contributed from Aoteroa/New Zealand

INGREDIENTS

40g butter

40g all-purpose flour

200ml chicken stock

225ml milk

2-3 cups cooked chicken

1 cup peas (frozen is fine)

5 cooked carrots

1 courgette

2 sheets of puff pastry (or three, if you have a large dish)

POTATO TOPPED CHICKEN AND MUSHOOM PIE

MAIN

Serves 2-4

Recipe contributed from the UK

60 minutes

DIRECTIONS

1. Preheat the oven to 220 °C/420 °F.
2. Fill a saucepan with water and bring to the boil.
3. Roughly slice the potatoes and add to saucepan, boil for approximately 10 minutes or until soft.
4. Heat oil in an oven-proof frying pan/cast iron pan.
5. Chop onions, peppers, mushrooms and carrot into chunks and put to one side.
6. Dice the chicken and bacon and add to the hot pan.
7. Season the chicken and bacon with mixed herbs, salt and black pepper.
8. Once the chicken is cooked through add the chopped vegetables and garlic until the veg have slightly softened.
9. Add the soup and peas.
10. Stir until everything is covered.
11. Layer potatoes on top of soupy mix, add as much panko as preferred and season with black pepper.
12. Put pan in preheated oven for approx. 25 mins or until panko is golden brown.
13. Serve (we usually serve with Yorkshire puds).

INGREDIENTS

1 large chicken breast or 2 boneless chicken thighs

1 or 2 rashers of bacon (as preferred)

1 red onion

1 green or red pepper

2 large flat mushrooms

1 large carrot

1 tin cream of mushroom soup

4 medium potatoes

1 tablespoon chopped garlic

1 teaspoon oil (of your choice)

Salt and black pepper to season

Mixed Herbs to season

Peas (as many as you like)

Panko breadcrumbs

NOTES

An oven-proof frying pan or cast iron pan is needed as the pan will be going into the oven. Serves 2 alone, 4 with sides. Can be topped with puff pastry instead of potatoes, cooking time remains the same.

ABOUT

This is a recipe for those who, like me, love pie but are pretty clueless in the kitchen. This is a rough recipe with a couple of cheats (like using tinned soup to make a sauce) and is open to adaptation. It has gone through a couple of different versions over the years but this is our favourite and is eaten weekly autumn through to spring - Laura Collins

CHIGNITION PEAR BURGER

MAIN

DIRECTIONS

1. Whack your patties into the oven, as per the packet instructions.
2. Cut your burger patties in half and set aside.
3. Wash and dry your lettuce, tomato and pear.
4. Prep the salad fillings: lay out your lettuce leaves (cutting off any stem bits), 1-2 per burger.
5. Slice your tomato, and lay half the slices on each lettuce pile.
6. Slice the pear, and set aside.
7. Slice the brie into ½ inch thick slices (around 1.3 cm) and set aside.
8. When the patties have two minutes left, top each patty with the sliced brie. Leave in the oven to get good and melty.
9. Add the brioche buns to the oven (in a rack above the patties) to toast. Watch them very carefully!
10. Pull everything out of the oven when the timer goes off.
11. Butter the base of the bun, and slather in garlic aioli. Place the lettuce and tomato on top, and the burger patty/cheese.
12. Butter the top bun, and add a good dollop of cranberry sauce,
13. Add the sliced pear to the lower and add the top bun.
14. Serve with fries.

Serves 2

30-50 minutes

Recipe contributed from Aoteroa/New Zealand

INGREDIENTS

2 seeded brioche burger buns

2 chicken buttermilk burger patties

2 tablespoons cranberry sauce

2 tablespoons garlic aioli

2-4 leaves greenbutter/boston lettuce

80g brie

1 pear

1 large tomato

NOTES

For ease this recipe uses premade chicken burger patties, but you could make your own. A fried egg or bacon make good additions!.

ABOUT

Burgerfuel, an amazing burger place in NZ, used to have a version of this burger, which was DELICIOUS. It quietly left it's menu in the mid 2000's. This is a tribute to afternoons in Mission Bay, with strawberry thick shakes and burgers on the beach.

HASSELBACK CHICKEN

MAIN

Serves 4

Recipe contributed from Australia

30 minutes

DIRECTIONS

1. Preheat the oven to fan 180 °C/350 °F.
2. Cut slashes into the chicken breasts widthways, about 2cm/1 inch apart. Cut about two-thirds through the chicken – you don't want to cut all the way.
3. Add a thin slice of mozzarella, a thin slice of tomato and a basil leaf to each cut and add to a baking tray.
4. Season and drizzle with olive oil.
5. Bake for 15-20 minutes until the chicken is cooked and the cheese has melted.
6. Drizzle over the pesto and a few more basil leaves.
7. Serve with a green salad and pasta or potatoes.

INGREDIENTS

4 skinless chicken breasts

1 ball mozzarella, thinly sliced

4 sun-dried tomatoes, sliced

a handful of basil leaves

olive oil

4 tablespoons fresh pesto

NOTES

A very easy traybake, perfect for a quick midweek meal that's easily doubled or halved. Great for impressing at dinner parties!

TURKEY, AVO + TORTILLA BAKE

MAIN

Serves 6

Recipe contributed from the UK

45 minutes

DIRECTIONS

1. Preheat the oven to fan 180 °C/350 °F.
2. Add celery and spring onions into a large bowl, and add mayonnaise with half the lemon juice and two-thirds of the grated cheese.
3. Season with salt and pepper, and toss to combine.
4. Toss the avocado cubes in the remaining lemon juice and add to the bowl with the turkey, tomatoes and parsley.
5. Carefully mix together and then spoon into a 1.1 litre, wide-based shallow ovenproof dish.
6. Scatter with the remaining cheese and the crushed tortilla chips and sprinkle with paprika.
7. Bake in the oven for 30-35 minutes until golden and piping hot in the middle. Do not allow it to boil (as it will separate).
8. Serve straight from the oven.

INGREDIENTS

2 celery sticks, thinly sliced

4 spring/green onions, sliced

300ml/10floz full fat mayonnaise

juice of one lemon

100g/4oz grated cheddar cheese

1 avocado, cubed

350g/12oz cooked turkey, cubed

300g/11oz cherry tomatoes

2 tablespoons chopped parsley

30g salted tortilla chips, crushed

paprika for sprinkling

salt and pepper.

NOTES

Great for using up leftover turkey or chicken! Can be made ahead, which makes for a very easy dinner. Make sure you use an avocado that is firm and just ripe, else the cubes will not keep their shape.

TURKEY VEG LASAGNE

MAIN

Serves 8-10

Recipe contributed from the UK

90 minutes

DIRECTIONS

1. Preheat the oven to fan 180 °C/350 °F.
2. Roughly chop the carrots, courgettes, cauliflower and aubergine, add to baking tray and roast till cooked through, around 20-25 minutes.
3. In the meantime, in a large pot over medium heat, add the minced garlic cloves with some olive oil, and cook until fragrant (maybe a minute or two).≠
4. Add the mince and fry until cooked through.
5. Once the roasted vegetables are done, add to a blender or food processor and blend until mostly smooth.
6. Once the turkey is properly cooked, no pink bits, add the passata, tomato paste, crumbled chicken stock cube, dried oregano, basil, peas and pureed roast veg to the pot and mix well to combine.
7. In a large lasagne dish, add a thin layer to the bottom, and place the dried lasagne sheets on top, breaking them if needed to ensure the dish is covered in a single layer.
8. Add a third of the turkey mince, and layer a third of the béchamel sauce on top, with a sprinkling of cheddar.
9. Add a layer of lasagne sheets, turkey mix, béchamel sauce and cheese.
10. On the last layer, add whole cherry tomatoes to the turkey mince layer before adding the béchamel sauce on top.
11. Top with the remaining cheddar. Rip the mozzarella and dot on top.
12. Bake 30-45 minutes, or until the lasagne sheets are soft and the cheese golden and bubbly.

INGREDIENTS

2 carrots

2 courgettes

½ head of cauliflower

1 aubergine/eggplant

1 tablespoon olive oil

3-4 garlic cloves, minced

500g turkey mince

700g passata

1 chicken stock cube

3 tablespoons tomato paste

2 teaspoons dried oregano

2 teaspoons dried basil

1 cup frozen peas

800g white béchamel sauce

handful cherry tomatoes

150g dried lasagne sheets

2-3 cups of grated cheddar

250g mozzarella

CHICKEN LASAGNE

MAIN

Serves 8-10

90 minutes

Recipe contributed from Aoteroa/New Zealand

DIRECTIONS

CHICKEN:

1. Place milk, broth and stock powder in a large saucepan. Bring to a very gentle simmer over medium heat, add chicken, pepper, bay leaves and thyme.
2. Cover with lid, simmer gently on medium-low for 15 minutes
3. Remove chicken and shred. Cover pot and set liquid aside.

MUSHROOMS:

4. Heat half the oil and butter in a large pot. Add half the mushrooms with half the garlic, salt and pepper.
5. Cook for 5 minutes, stirring leisurely, until golden. Transfer to bowl and repeat with remaining mushrooms.

WHITE SAUCE:

6. Lower heat to medium. Melt butter in skillet, then add garlic.
7. Stir until golden.
8. Add flour. Stir constantly for 1 minute. Gradually pour in 2 cups of reserved poaching liquid while stirring constantly.
9. Mix in another cup of liquid, then remaining liquid and stir well to dissolve, whisking to make lump free.
10. Stir constantly for 1 to 2 minutes until it thickens.
11. Remove from heat, stir in cheese until melted and season.
12. REMOVE 2 1/2 cups of sauce (save for topping). Then stir in chicken and mushrooms into remaining sauce.

ASSEMBLE & BAKE:

13. Preheat oven to 180°C/350°F.
14. Cover base of 23 x 33 cm / 9 x 13" baking dish with lasagne sheets. Alternate sheets with chicken mixture.
15. Pour over reserved White Sauce, sprinkle with mozzarella.
16. Cover loosely with foil or use upside down baking tray.
17. Bake for 25 minutes. Remove foil, bake further 10 minutes til golden and bubbly.
18. Stand 10 minutes, before serving.

INGREDIENTS

CHICKEN:

2kg/2lb chicken breast or boneless skinless thigh

4 cups milk

4 cups chicken broth / stock

2 bay leaves, dried

3 sprigs thyme

1 chicken stock cube

½ teaspoon black pepper

MUSHROOMS:

30g butter

2 tablespoons olive oil

500g/1lb mushrooms, quartered

2 garlic cloves, minced

½ teaspoon salt and pepper, each

WHITE SAUCE:

30g butter

2 garlic cloves, minced

110g plain flour

2 cups grated cheddar cheese

LASAGNE:

375g/13oz fresh lasagne sheets

200g/7oz mozzarella cheese, shredded

IRANIAN CHICKEN WITH SPICED YOGHURT

MAIN

DIRECTIONS

1. Preheat oven to 200°C/395 °F (fan 180 °C/350 °F).
2. Line a large roasting tin with non-stick baking paper. Divide the chicken legs into drumsticks and thighs by cutting through the joint with a sharp knife. Put in a large mixing bowl.
3. In a small mixing bowl, mix the spices with the olive oil, honey, lemon zest and juice and some salt and pepper. Pour over the chicken and toss well to coat all over.
4. Put the chicken in the prepared roasting tin and roast for 45 minutes until golden and tender, turning halfway through and basting the chicken with pan juices.
5. Put the chicken on a board (or platter if serving straightaway) to cool.
6. Put 2 tablespoons of the pan juices in a bowl with the yogurt, then mix well and season to taste.
7. To serve, drizzle the yogurt over the chicken and scatter with parsley.

Serves 6

10 minutes prep
50 minutes cooking

Recipe contributed from the UK

INGREDIENTS

6 skin-on chicken legs

6 cardamom pods, seeds removed and ground in a pestle and mortar or spice grinder

1 teaspoon ground cinnamon

1 teaspoon ground turmeric

½ teaspoon ground cumin

2 tablespoons olive oil

2 teaspoons clear honey

Grated zest and juice 1 lemon

150ml greek yoghurt

Handful fresh parsley, roughly chopped

ABOUT

Bolognese, everyone has a recipe, and few of them resemble anything you'd ever find on an Italian menu. In reality, this is a meat ragu recipe from northern Italy. You'll find as many variants as there are Italian regions. The key is having a mix of lean beef (or lamb in a pinch) and fatty pork. The second most important ingredient is time, a good 'Bol' takes time, but it's not very labour-intensive. Pour a glass of wine, stick on a movie and enjoy the fragrant perfume of bol coming together over 4-5 hours. Make a large batch, and know you've got a quick and tasty meal on hand for weeks to come.This should make oodles of Bol, it keeps really well in the freezer and is quick to reheat as a freezer meal that will always put a smile on your face.

THE DOM HARRIS BOLOGNESE

MAIN

DIRECTIONS

1. Heat oil in a large (5-6L) saucepan over medium heat, add onions, carrot and celery and cook, stirring regularly until onion is translucent, but not brown.
2. Crush 2-3 cloves of garlic into the veg. You can also add some mixed/Italian herbs
3. Raise the temperature to medium high and add the meat, half a pack at a time, stir infrequently, enough to prevent sticking but let the meat brown. Crumble over a beef stock cube for extra flavour.
4. Whilst this is happening add stock cubes to boiling water in a separate pan,or heat pre-made stock. stock should be warm but not boiling.
5. As the meat browns you'll end up with a fair bit of liquid in your pan, keep stirring until most of this has evaporated.
6. Lower the heat to low-medium and add a couple of ladles of stock into the meat, it should just cover the meat and blip away but not be boiling. Stir every 15-20 minutes adding a ladle or two of stock to keep the level up. This stage can take 90 minutes or more.
7. Optional - once you've cooked away the last of the stock, you can do a final top-up with a large glass of red or white wine.
8. Once most of the remaining liquid has reduced, add one can of chopped tomatoes, the rest of the crushed garlic, bay leaves and tomato puree. Remember, this is a meat sauce, not a tomato one, so the sauce shouldn't be too moist, but depending on how much liquid is in the tinned tomatoes, you may need 2 tins of tomatoes.
9. Keep the heat low-medium, and let the bol blip away for another hour or two, stirring every 20 minutes, until there's not a huge amount of liquid, some of the fat has separated and the sauce looks silky.

11. If you must, you can skim off and dispose of some of the fat, although fat is flavour. Best leave it.

Serves many

4-5 hours

Recipe contributed from the UK

INGREDIENTS

3 tablespoons olive oil

2 medium onions - finely diced

1 carrot - finely diced

1-2 celery stalks - peeled to remove string and finely diced

½ head of garlic

500g pork mince

500g lean beef mince

1 tin chopped tomatoes

50g tomato puree

2 bay leaves

mixed herbs

beef stock cube

1½ litre chicken or veggie stock

Optional - 1 glass of red or white wine

Phe and Dom Harris, good friends of Elly + Sam <3 x

THE BAVETTE

MAIN

DIRECTIONS

1. Add the brine ingredients to 1 litre of cold water in a large saucepan that isn't going to react badly to the salt.
2. Boil and stir until the ingredients dissolve, then allow to cool completely.
3. Immerse the Bavette in the cold brine and cover for 1 hour, try not to exceed 90mins of brining time as it can make the meat overly salty.
4. Drain and transfer the Bavette to a clean bowl, then combine the Marinade ingredients and mix thoroughly.
5. Leave for at least 1 hour to marinate, ideally place in a fridge overnight.
6. Remove the Bavette from the fridge and bring up to room temperature, usually 1 hour before cooking. Turn on your oven to 90°C/195 °F (yes, low), and prepare a large roasting tray, and a large grilling pan, preferably an iron skillet but a large nonstick frying pan will do.
7. Remove the Bavette from the marinade, keeping as little oil on the meat as possible.
8. Place in a large roasting pan in the oven for 30mins. Then remove from the roasting tray, liberally salt the meat, and grill in a smoking hot pan for 2 minutes per side.
9. Rest for 10mins, cut into 2cm slices across the grain of the meat, and serve.

NOTES

The goal of this recipe is to get tender Bavette, a cheaper cut of meat, that is more delicious than an expensive steak and suitable for group dining. The reverse sear method is a fairly foolproof method of not over or under-cooking the meat. Salting the meat right before searing it helps give it the cooked crust which is much of the delicious flavour of grilled steak. You can use black pepper if you like. Always cut Bavette across the grain, else it could be chewy.

Serves 6

90 minutes

Recipe contributed from the UK

INGREDIENTS

400g per person of Bavette or Flank steak; this recipe is scaled to 1kg

BRINE

100g sea salt

50g brown sugar

1 tablespoon treacle, golden syrup, or honey

2 bay leaves

8 peppercorns

8 cloves

MARINADE:

100ml vegetable oil

4 garlic cloves, chopped

1 small-medium chilli, chopped

1 lemon, zested

2 tablespoon thyme, chopped

Dan, Bex and Wilf Chaffleson, also, good friends of Elly + Sam <3 x

BBQ BRISKET ON THE BONE FOR 30

MAIN

DIRECTIONS

1. Make the rub. Grind everything, except the salt, together in a pestle and mortar until the pepper is roughly ground, then add the salt and mix it in (don't grind) with the rest.
2. Liberally apply to the meat with your hands, rubbing it in.
3. Leave the meat, covered, in a cool place overnight.
4. The following morning, get the meat in the kitchen to raise the temperature a little - don't cook cold meat!
5. Put the chopped vegetables in the bottom of a large roasting tray and place the meat on top.
6. Place any dry rub left on top of the joint.
7. Add enough beer and water to cover the base without immersing the meat. Wrap the top of the roasting dish in foil to make it steam-tight.
8. This is cooked via the indirect method on the BBQ. Suggest the coals are lit an hour before you want to cook. Nominally, you want the temperature to be 180 - 200 C before you start cooking. Place the roasting dish on the grill ensuring that it is not exposed to direct heat and place the lid on your BBQ. Keep the temperature above 140 C after the first hour, checking the fuel every couple of hours.
   DO NOT unseal the meat for the first 6 hours! At 6 hours, check the temperature of the meat using a meat thermometer.
9. Looking for a temperature around 80 - 90 C. If it needs more cooking, wrap it up and leave it for another hour or two.
10. Once the meat is at 80 - 90 C, take it out of the meat dish and place it directly on the BBQ grill. After 40-45 minutes you should have some great colour on the meat.
11. Take it off the heat and let it rest for at least an hour, wrapped in foil. The meat juices and vegetables can be reserved to make an amazing gravy.

Serves 30

30 minutes prep +
6 - 10 hours to cook

Recipe contributed
from the UK

INGREDIENTS

7 - 8 kg beef brisket on the bone

400-500ml beer

For the dry rub:

1 tablespoon peppercorns

1 tablespoon ground cumin

1 teaspoon ground cloves

1 teaspoon turmeric

1 tablespoon sea salt

If you want to try something a bit different, add 2 teaspoons ground coriander and chilli powder to the dry rub.

Veg for the roasting tray:

onions, carrots, celery - chopped roughly - enough to cover the bottom of your roasting pan.

ABOUT

Recipe submitted by Tony Collins, Mikaere Foundation Trustee. The recipe will work best on a kettle BBQ. There are no exact timings. Patience and several beers will help! This was first cooked for the fundraising BarBeKai. Tony made it up as he went along - and had no complaints!

SAM'S SZECHUAN BEEF

MAIN

Serves 4

Recipe contributed from the UK

25 minutes

DIRECTIONS

1. Combine the mirin and soy sauce and then mix with the cornstarch, add the beef and toss/massage to coat the meat.
2. Let meat marinate for at least 10 minutes.
3. In a medium mixing bowl, whisk together sauce ingredients and set aside.
4. Add sesame oil to wok (or large frying pan) and heat over medium to high heat.
5. Add beef to the hot pan and fry until just nearly cooked.
6. Pour in Szechuan sauce, turn to coat the meat and cook for an extra minute or two, it'll mix with the cornstarch and become slightly thickened.
7. Serve over rice.

INGREDIENTS

for the beef:

17.5oz/500g sliced beef

1 tablespoon soy sauce

1 tablespoon mirin

3 dessert spoons cornstarch

3 tablespoons sesame oil

for the sauce:

1 teaspoon crushed red pepper flakes

1 teaspoon Chinese 5 spice

4 tablespoons soy sauce

2 tablespoons packed brown sugar

2 cloves garlic - minced

1 inch of fresh ginger - grated or very finely minced

2 tablespoons water

1 tablespoon Sriracha

1 tablespoon rice wine vinegar

2 tablespoons of bbq sauce

1 green onion - thinly sliced for garnish

NOTES

Not much beats the smell of sesame oil as it warms, but if you don't have this you can substitute with olive oil instead. When frying the beef, add in any other veg you might fancy, sliced red peppers etc.

OVEN SLOW ROAST BRISKET

MAIN

Serves 4

Recipe contributed from Aoteroa/ New Zealand

5 min prep, 2-24 hours curing, 4 hours cooking and resting.

DIRECTIONS

1. Dry the brisket with paper towels, and rub on all sides with spices, Worcestershire sauce and salt. A store-bought Moroccan Spice mix is perfect if you're unsure. Leave covered overnight, or at minimum for 2-3 hours. Longer the better, but don't do less than 2 hours before cooking or the meat will dry too much.
2. Prior to cooking, sit it on the bench till it reaches room temperature. Preheat oven to 125°C.
3. Roast covered in foil, fat side up, for 3 hours in the middle of oven. Note: Cooking guidelines are 1 hour per 500g of meat.
4. Mix BBQ sauce and sugar in a small bowl.
5. Remove brisket from the oven, cover generously in sauce and put back in the oven, uncovered, for 30 minutes.
6. Remove from oven, lightly cover with foil and sit on the bench for 20-30 minutes to rest.
7. Slice into finger-width strips. Always slice it against the grain.

INGREDIENTS

1.5kg brisket

2-3 tablespoons spices of choice

2 teaspoons salt

2 tablespoons Worcestershire sauce

250ml BBQ sauce

¼ cup brown sugar

ABOUT

This is recipe is contributed by Andrew Day, who has evolved this recipe from his personal experience cooking brisket. Andrew and Elly have been friends for decades, and Andrew says he's "Just a Kai super-fan <3"

STUFFED SHELLS

MAIN

DIRECTIONS

1. For the sauce: In a large Dutch oven or pot, heat the olive oil over medium heat. Add onion and a pinch of salt and cook, stirring occasionally, until softened, 5 to 7 minutes.
2. Add the garlic and tomato purée, stirring frequently, about 2 minutes.
3. Stir in the pasta sauce, season with salt, and then bring to a simmer. Cover halfway and cook, stirring occasionally, until the sauce has thickened slightly, 30 minutes.
4. Preheat oven to 190 °C/375 °F.
5. Now is a good time to cook the spinach, if you need to. Squeeze as much water out of the spinach as possible.
6. Bring a large pot of salted water to a boil.
7. In a medium bowl, combine the ricotta with 1½ cups mozzarella, 1 cup Parmesan, cooked spinach and egg yolks.
8. Grate the garlic directly into the bowl, then season with 1 teaspoon salt and ½ teaspoon pepper. Stir to combine.
9. Add the shells to the boiling water and cook until just shy of al dente. (Cook the shells for about 2 minutes less than the minimum time listed on the package)
10. Reserve ½ cup pasta water, then drain the pasta and rinse it under cold water to cool. Count out 24 shells. (You'll have cooked more shells than will fit in the dish; just in case any rip.)
11. Stir the pasta water into the sauce, then add half the sauce to a 9-by-13-inch baking dish and spread it in an even layer.
12. Spoon about 2 tablespoons of filling into each of the 24 shells, lining up the stuffed shells in the dish as you go. Spoon the remaining sauce over the shells, then sprinkle with the remaining 1 cup mozzarella and 1 cup Parmesan.
13. Cover the dish tightly with foil and bake for 30 minutes.
14. Remove the foil and bake, uncovered, for another 15 to 20 minutes till the cheese is golden and bubbly.

Serves 6-8

2 hours

Recipe contributed from the UK

INGREDIENTS

SAUCE

¼ cup extra-virgin olive oil

1 medium onion, finely chopped

4 garlic cloves, peeled and thinly sliced

3 tablespoons tomato purée (tomato paste in the US)

2x400g/1x28oz can tomato pasta sauce (tomato purée in the US)

FILLING + ASSEMBLY

450g/1lb/2 cups fresh ricotta

2 cups cooked spinach

283g/10oz/2½ cups mozzarella, grated

155g/5½oz/2 cups Parmesan, freshly and finely grated

2 egg yolks

1 garlic clove

340g/12oz jumbo shells

QUORN AND ALE CASSEROLE

MAIN

Serves 2-4

Recipe contributed from the UK

40 minutes

DIRECTIONS

1. Heat the oil in a heavy casserole dish or saucepan and gently fry the onion and garlic until golden.
2. Add the Quorn chunks, sliced carrots, grated nutmeg, sugar, bayleaf, mushrooms and ale.
3. Bring to the boil, then reduce to a simmer and put on the lid.
4. Leave for approximately 30 minutes, until the carrots are tender.
5. Use a thickening agent such as 2-3 teaspoons of cornflour mixed to a paste with water, to give you a nice hearty casserole. Season to taste.
6. Serve with crispy skinned baked potatoes and a green vegetable, for an easy and satisfying vegetarian meal. Perfect for the colder months.

INGREDIENTS

1 tablespoon olive oil

200g/7oz pack of Quorn chunks

1 medium onion, chopped

1 clove garlic, crushed

½ pint/275ml brown ale (I use Newcastle Brown)

Salt and pepper

Nutmeg, approx quarter teaspoon, freshly grated

Bayleaf

1 teaspoon sugar

2-3 carrots, sliced

thickening agent (like 2-3 teaspoons of cornflour)

225g/8oz pack of chestnut or button mushrooms, quartered if large

NOTES

Quorn is not suitable for vegans as it contains egg. There are plenty of vegan alternatives that you can use. You can also substitute other ingredients, such as whole baby shallots instead of onions and other root vegetables in place of carrots. Just use what you've got.

ABOUT

Submitted by Sue. This is a Choules family recipe, adapted from a meat recipe (Flemish Beef) given to me by my sister Wendy (Mikaere's Grandma) many years ago (before I was vegetarian). I loved it, so tweaked it a bit when I gave up meat. There's nothing like a warming, hearty stew on a cold day. If you're looking to cut down the amount of meat you eat, then try this vegetarian version. The brown ale gives it a deep, rich flavour and you can add lots of vegetables to make it extra healthy.

SAM'S MAC AND CHEESE

MAIN

DIRECTIONS

1. Grate all the cheese
2. Melt the butter into a large saucepan – chop up the garlic and throw that in too
3. Once the garlic is browned it's time to make a roux, sieve in the flour and stir til combined
4. Put heat to medium and keep stirring until you get a paste which should happen pretty quickly
5. Start adding the milk a little at a time, and whisk in making sure there are no lumps (except garlic lumps)
6. Once the milk has been added, it'll be looking pretty watery.
7. Turn the heat up and get it to a soft boil. Keep stirring, once it's at a boil it'll get thicker so turn it down to a simmer – keep stirring intermittently. Add the grated cheese (keep some back for the topping), stir until all the cheese has melted. Taste and season as you like.
8. Turn on the grill and get your pasta cooking, as per the packet instructions
9. Once the pasta is cooked, drain and add the cheese sauce.
10. Add other ingredients at this point (I like cherry tomatoes), stir and add to a baking dish
11. Throw the last of the cheese on top and place under the warmed grill, till the cheese on top is just crispy and golden, but the sauce is still runny with the pasta - bloody lovely.
12. Serve immediately with a side salad.

Serves 4

60 minutes

Recipe contributed from the UK

INGREDIENTS

5 cloves of garlic

50g butter

3 heaped dessert spoons plain flour

750ml of milk

500g dried spiral pasta (like fusilloni or cavatappi. Macaroni if you must)

350g cheddar cheese

175g red Leicester cheese

Any vegetable additions (cherry tomatoes, peas, corn, wilted spinach, courgettes, cooked carrots etc)

ABOUT

Sam's wife Elly LOVES mac and cheese. So Sam developed this dish, perfecting it over the years. It's proper good, and great for dinner parties.

BARBARA'S SPINACH + FETA PIE

MAIN

Serves 4-6

Recipe contributed from Aoteroa/New Zealand

60 minutes

DIRECTIONS

1. Preheat the oven to fan 180 °C/350 °F.
2. If your additional vege requires cooking, do that now (vege like peas and courgettes are probably fine frozen/raw because they'll cook in the pie, but you'd probably want to cook anything like sweet potato/broccoli etc)
3. Defrost the spinach, and squeeze as much water out as possible (I like to wrap it in a teatowel and twist, squeezing out all the liquid).
4. Drain the sundried tomatoes, and chop.
5. In a bowl, mix the spinach, sundried tomatoes, and any additional vege you fancy adding.
6. Crumble the feta cheese into the mix and stir.
7. Grease your pie dish, and line with a sheet of pastry.
8. Pour in your spinach mix, and spread evenly over the bottom.
9. In a bowl, beat your eggs and season.
10. Pour over the spinach mix, and top with the second puff pastry sheet.
11. Bake till the egg is cooked, around 45 minutes.

INGREDIENTS

2 frozen packs of spinach

1 pack of feta

2 puff pastry sheets

12 eggs

½ jar of sundried tomatoes

Any other vege you fancy throwing in (courgettes, peas, sweet potato cubes, broccoli etc)

NOTES

This recipe is very robust and very easy to make. Can be made in muffin tins (as shown) or as a regular pie (as per the recipe). It's delicious and amazing.

ABOUT

Barbara Ward is a sculptural artist turned electorate secretary for NZ's Prime Minister. Many, many years ago she shared this recipe with Elly (very kindly omitting the onion), and it's been a firm favourite ever since!

CRUSTLESS COURGETTE QUICHE

MAIN

Serves 4-6

35 minutes

Recipe contributed from Aoteroa/New Zealand

INGREDIENTS

4-5 Courgettes grated

5 eggs

Add as many other ingredients as you like - onions (grated or chopped), bacon (chopped), cheese (grated), feta, spinach, capsicum etc

1 cup self raising flour

½ cup oil

Salt/Pepper

DIRECTIONS

1. Preheat oven to 180°C/ 355°C.
2. Mix all ingredients together and add to a quiche dish
3. Bake till golden brown, about 30 mins.

ABOUT

This is recipe is contributed by Kat O'Leary, a wonderful, wonderful friend of Elly. They've been friends for almost 20 years! She's always been an avid baker/chef. I still remember when she introduced me to water chestnuts in an amazing home cooked Asian dish, and I can't help but think of her when I have them now!

P
S

PERFECT PUTTANESCA

MAIN

Serves 4

Recipe contributed from the UK

25 minutes

DIRECTIONS

1. Salt a pan full of water for the pasta and bring to a boil.
2. Drain the oil from the anchovies into a frying pan and set the anchovies aside.
3. Finely chop the garlic and cherry tomatoes and add to the oil in the pan.
4. Cook on a medium temperature for one minute, then add the chilli flakes.
5. Stir, then add the tomato purée. After another minute, add the tin of tomatoes.
6. Your pasta water should now be boiling. Add the pasta and cook according to the packet instructions.
7. Whilst the pasta is cooking, add the olives, capers and pinch of sugar to the sauce. Leave to simmer until the pasta is one minute away from being cooked.
8. With a ladle, remove a couple tablespoons of pasta water and add to the sauce mix to loosen it up.
9. At the same time, add the anchovies. They should break up in the sauce and only need a few seconds to heat up.
10. Drain the pasta and stir into the sauce.
11. Season to taste and serve up with the fresh parsley on top.

INGREDIENTS

320g linguine

1 pack of fresh anchovies

2 cloves of garlic

1 pinch of chilli flakes

1 teaspoon tomato purée

1 tin of chopped tomatoes

10 cherry tomatoes

A handful of black olives

1 tablespoon of capers

1 pinch of caster sugar

A handful of fresh, chopped parsley

ABOUT

This recipe was submitted and illustrated by Zoë Ellison, who illustrated Charlie the Crow - one of the children's books whose royalties support NKH Research.

CHEAT'S RATATOUILLE

MAIN

Serves 4-6

Recipe contributed from the UK

10 minutes prep, 60 minutes to cook

DIRECTIONS

1. Preheat the oven to 200 °C/395 °F (or fan 180 °C/350 °F).
2. Slice the courgette as thinly as you can be bothered - I use the long blade on a cheese grater.
3. Slice the aubergine into thin half-moons.
4. Halve, and then quarter the red onions.
5. Chop the peppers into small chunks.
6. Mince the garlic.
7. Chop or tear the basil.
8. Combine the breadcrumbs and the parmesan, and set aside
9. Add all of the veggies, garlic and basil into a roasting dish, add the olive oil, liberally salt and pepper the dish, and mix thoroughly. It's fine if it's quite full, it will cook down quite a bit.
10. Pour the tins of tomatoes over the top and smush it around so it covers the whole dish.
11. Put in the oven for 30 mins.
12. Remove from the oven, give the veggies a gentle stir, and then sprinkle the parmesan breadcrumbs over the top of the dish. Return to the oven for another 30 mins.
13. Remove and let it sit for 5-10 mins before serving.

INGREDIENTS

2 400g tins tomatoes

2 aubergines

3 courgettes

3 peppers, red or orange

2 red onions

3 cloves of garlic

2 tablespoons olive oil

30g fresh basil (one big bunch)

30g grated parmesan

75g breadcrumbs

sea salt black pepper

NOTES

This is a really robust recipe, so you can increase/decrease the veg to suit your taste or tray size. The quantities above fit comfortably in a standard roasting tin. If you don't have fresh basil, dried works. You can add any other herbs you like as well - a bit of rosemary is really good. Great on its own with good bread, but also makes a good side with herby chicken. It's also more delicious the next day, and can be turned into a pasta bake really easily - just heat it, add another tin of tomatoes, and pasta. Grate some cheese on top and put it in the oven for about 15 mins. I normally add bacon or chorizo too! Recipe submitted by the brilliant Emma Coley <3

EASY PIZZA DOUGH

MAIN

Serves 2

90 minutes

Recipe contributed from Aoteroa

DIRECTIONS

1. Mix water, yeast, sugar and 1 handful of flour in a large mixing bowl, and stand for 5 minutes (until frothy).
2. Mix in the flour, salt and oil with a round-bladed knife.
3. Keep mixing till it looks like a shaggy mess.
4. Sprinkle with flour and knead on the bench for 10 minutes.
5. Sprinkle more flour at intervals as required until it doesn't stick to your hands and come apart. The dough should be smooth as you knead it.
6. Transfer to an oiled bowl, cover with a plate or wet cloth and let rise for 30-60 minutes (until doubled in size).
7. Turn onto a floured surface and knock the air out of it with your hands. Portion into two, and roll into balls.
8. If preparing in advance, keep it covered in the fridge. If cooking immediately, preheat the oven to 200 °C/395 °F.
9. Stretch each ball out over your hands until in a 25cm disc with slightly thicker edges.
10. Add toppings of choice and bake for 8 minutes. A pizza tray on a hot stone in the centre of the oven is a great method.

INGREDIENTS

400g 00 grade (fine) bread flour

250ml warm water

7g active Yeast

2 teaspoon sugar

1-2 teaspoon ground rock salt

2 tablespoon olive oil

NOTES

You can easily multiply the recipe for more pizzas, and play around with the water and flour as different flours require more/less water and oil. If using a normal all-purpose flour, try adding 2 Tbsp of gluten powder to increase pliability.

ABOUT

Recipe submitted by Andrew Day. I created this from a number of recipes I've read and been given verbally. This one works best with the most consistent dough, considering I'm not a base-tossing professional pizza chef.

ELLY'S FLUFFY PANCAKES

BREAKFAST

Serves 4

90 minutes

Recipe contributed from Aoteroa

DIRECTIONS

1. In a large bowl, mix the flour, baking powder, salt and caster sugar.
2. In a separate jug, whisk together the milk and egg and melted butter
3. Pour the milk mixture into the flour mixture and beat until you have a smooth batter, without any lumps.
4. Let the batter stand for a few minutes.
5. Heat a non-stick frying pan over medium heat and add a knob of butter. When it's melted, add a tablespoon of batter (do not thin the batter, it should seem very thick).
6. When the top begins to bubble, flip it over and cook until both sides are golden brown.
7. Repeat till the batter is gone and you have a stack of pancakes. I tend to keep them on a warmed plate covered with a tea towel.
8. Serve with berries, lemon and sugar, or maple syrup and fruit.

INGREDIENTS

135g/4¾oz plain flour

1 teaspoon baking powder

½ teaspoon salt

2 tablespoons caster sugar

130ml/4½fl oz milk

1 large egg, lightly beaten

2 tablespoons melted butter

NOTES

This recipe is SO easy to make and produces super fluffy pancakes. If you're feeling fancy, throw in a handful of crushed blueberries or chocolate chips to change it up.

If you're feeling really fancy, while the batter is standing, stew an apple or two: peel, core and thinly slice your apples, and add to a small pot with 1 tablespoon each of brown sugar, lemon juice and water. Add ½ teaspoon of ground cinnamon and give it a good stir. Cover and heat on medium heat for 5-15 minutes. It takes minutes and it is LUSH on top of pancakes! I usually also serve a fruit bowl/board for people to help themselves with whatever fruit I have on hand: bananas, blueberries, strawberries, peaches, pears, plums etc. Delicious!

QUINOA PORRIDGE

BREAKFAST

Serves 4

30 minutes

Recipe contributed from Melborne, VIC, Australia

INGREDIENTS

1 cup quinoa

1 ½ cup water

1 cup coconut milk

1 tablespoon coconut yoghurt

Optional:

1-2 teaspoons maple syrup

Sprinkle of cinnamon

DIRECTIONS

1. Activate quinoa by rinsing in water and dry frying until you smell a nuttiness and the grains release their tendrils
2. Cook quinoa in water by bringing it to a boil and simmer on low heat for 12 minutes, fluff with a fork and leave with the lid on for a further 5 minutes.
3. Add coconut milk and yoghurt and cook on low for approximately 8 minutes until porridge consistency.
4. Top with dried fruit, and serve!

NOTES

I had to find alternative recipes when my little one presented with multiple food allergies. This one is a daily staple now and can be adapted for sweet or savoury. Refrigerate for up to 4 days.

ABOUT

Submitted by the amazing Emma Price, the most beautiful lady that she is. I'm so grateful for you, ladycakes <3 x

SIDES

MAMA HORTSMAN'S EASY BROCCOLI CASSEROLE

SIDE

DIRECTIONS

1. Preheat the oven to fan 180 °C/350 °F.
   Cook broccoli according to package instructions.
2. Set aside while you prep and allow to cool slightly, so that it's still warm but easily handled.
3. Combine 4 tablespoons of melted butter with flour, milk, and cream cheese. Salt too, if using.
4. Place cooked broccoli in a 9 x 13 pan or casserole dish, add the chopped onion.
5. Pour melted creamy topping over the broccoli-onion mixture.
6. Stir, to coat the broccoli.
7. Add cheese - on top or mixed in.
8. Bake for 25 minutes.
9. While baking, melt the remaining 4 tablespoons of butter and combine with bread crumbs.
10. After 25 minutes, remove dish and top with bread crumb mixture.
11. Bake for another 10 minutes.

ABOUT

When my family moved from Illinois to Pennsylvania, this recipe was shared with my mother by a mom's group she attended to meet new people. When we returned to Illinois, it continued to be a family favorite as a reminder of the warmth brought by a community of people coming together. We cherish it at holidays, and now whenever I'm asked to share a recipe, I think of this one. I hope your family will enjoy it as much as my family does. Submitted by Stephanie on behalf of Rhett's Rumble with NKH. Rhett is the sweetest 4 year old, from Chicago, IL. He loves clapping, kicking to make his rocker move, twinkle lights, and when his siblings sing to him!

Serves 8-12

45 minutes

Recipe contributed from the USA

INGREDIENTS

900g/2lb frozen cut broccoli

½ cup onion - rough chop or diced

8 tablespoons butter, melted

4 tablespoons flour

¼ teaspoon salt - optional

2 cups milk

225g/8oz cream cheese - room temp

225g/8oz cheddar cheese,

1 cup bread crumbs

NOTES

We've always used frozen broccoli for speed, but fresh steamed broccoli could easily be substituted.

SIDES

MAMA HORTSMAN'S EASY BROCCOLI CASSEROLE

SIDE

DIRECTIONS

1. Preheat the oven to fan 180 °C/350 °F.

   Cook broccoli according to package instructions.
2. Set aside while you prep and allow to cool slightly, so that it's still warm but easily handled.
3. Combine 4 tablespoons of melted butter with flour, milk, and cream cheese. Salt too, if using.
4. Place cooked broccoli in a 9 x 13 pan or casserole dish, add the chopped onion.
5. Pour melted creamy topping over the broccoli-onion mixture.
6. Stir, to coat the broccoli.
7. Add cheese - on top or mixed in.
8. Bake for 25 minutes.
9. While baking, melt the remaining 4 tablespoons of butter and combine with bread crumbs.
10. After 25 minutes, remove dish and top with bread crumb mixture.
11. Bake for another 10 minutes.

ABOUT

When my family moved from Illinois to Pennsylvania, this recipe was shared with my mother by a mom's group she attended to meet new people. When we returned to Illinois, it continued to be a family favorite as a reminder of the warmth brought by a community of people coming together. We cherish it at holidays, and now whenever I'm asked to share a recipe, I think of this one. I hope your family will enjoy it as much as my family does. Submitted by Stephanie on behalf of Rhett's Rumble with NKH. Rhett is the sweetest 4 year old, from Chicago, IL. He loves clapping, kicking to make his rocker move, twinkle lights, and when his siblings sing to him!

Serves 8-12

45 minutes

Recipe contributed from the USA

INGREDIENTS

900g/2lb frozen cut broccoli

½ cup onion - rough chop or diced

8 tablespoons butter, melted

4 tablespoons flour

¼ teaspoon salt - optional

2 cups milk

225g/8oz cream cheese - room temp

225g/8oz cheddar cheese,

1 cup bread crumbs

NOTES

We've always used frozen broccoli for speed, but fresh steamed broccoli could easily be substituted.

TRUFFLE CREAM COLESLAW

SIDE

Serves 6

20 minutes

Recipe contributed from the UK

DIRECTIONS

1. Assemble the dressing at least an hour (ideally more) before serving: combine crème fraîche, greek yoghurt, sour cream, dijon mustard, sweet paprika, hot paprika, Truff sauce, and salt in a large bowl.
2. Mix thoroughly and set aside in the fridge for the flavours to combine.
3. Wash and peel your carrots and remove the outer leaves of the cabbage and onion.
4. Grate the carrots into a bowl, finely chop your cabbages into slices 1-2mm thick and about 5cm long for a consistent texture coleslaw.
5. Finely slice the onion and combine all the vegetables in a bowl.
6. Add the dressing to the vegetables a scoop at a time and toss to coat, until you have an even coverage to the consistency you desire.
7. Any leftover dressing makes an excellent table sauce for other dishes.

INGREDIENTS

1 medium red onion

2 medium carrots

½ white cabbage

½ red cabbage

½ lemon, juice and zest

200ml crème fraîche

200ml greek yoghurt

150ml sour cream

1 tablespoon dijon mustard

2 teaspoon Truff hot sauce (truff.com)

1 teaspoon sweet paprika

½ teaspoon hot smoked paprika

1 teaspoon fine salt

NOTES

The vegetables may all be chopped in advance and stored in a bowl under cold water for several hours if required, ensure you thoroughly drain before using. The dressing may be balanced to taste by adding small quantities of any of salt, sweet paprika, dijon, lemon or Truff. Note that paprika and Truff have strong flavours, so add only a little at a time to balance. The lemon will also thin out the yoghurt, so add a little and stir it in to avoid separating the mixture - you want to achieve the consistency of thick pouring cream to best coat the coleslaw in the dressing. The hot paprika should be used sparingly as it can overpower other ingredients and leave a coarse burning flavour which doesn't mix well with the cream of the dressing. We use multiple types of soured cream and paprika to give depth to the flavour, but you could do the recipe with just the greek yoghurt and sweet paprika. This recipe was submitted by the Chafflesons, wonderful friends of Sam and Elly. Modified from a typical American cream coleslaw recipe by Dan's good friend Charlotte Pawar.

POP UP SOUP ROLLS

SIDE

DIRECTIONS

1. Preheat oven to 230°C/450°F.
2. Spray a 6-cup muffin tin with non-stick cooking spray and set aside.
3. In a small bowl, add the flour and the sugar and blend. In another, add the milk and the mayo, and mix.
4. Add the dry mix to the wet until just combined - be careful not to over mix or they'll be tough.
5. Spoon the batter into 6 muffin cups
6. Bake until a toothpick comes out clean, about 12-14 minutes.
7. Cool for 5 minutes before removing from pan. Place on a wire rack to cool further.
8. Serve warm with soup!

Serves 6

20 minutes

Recipe contributed from the USA

INGREDIENTS

1 cup self-raising flour

½ cup semi-skimmed/2% milk

2 tablespoons mayonnaise

½ teaspoon sugar

NOTES

If you don't have self raising flour, you can use 1 cup of all purpose and 1½ teaspoons of baking powder. If you're feeling really fancy, you can add ½ teaspoon of rosemary and ½ teaspoon of garlic powder. Comes out light and fluffy, a mix between a biscuit/scone and a bread roll,

SIU MAI (CHINESE DUMPLINGS)

SIDE

DIRECTIONS

1. Soak your shiitake mushrooms for 20 minutes in a large bowl with boiling water. Squeeze out excess water and finely chop.
2. If you need to peel/devein/cook/dice your prawns, do that now. Also finely mince the white part of your spring onions.
3. Make the dipping sauce: Mix 3 parts soy, 1 part vinegar, and chilli to taste. Mix and set aside.
4. Place chicken, salt, soy sauce, rice wine and sugar in a large mixing bowl. Mix vigorously with a spoon.
5. Add mushrooms, prawns and spring onions, mix until just mixed. This is your filling.
6. Form an "O" with your forefinger and thumb. Place a wonton wrapper over the "O". Push in 1 heaped teaspoon of filling and push down into the "O" hole. Use a butter knife to smear more filling until the wonton is full.
7. Place on a flat surface and push down to flatten base and use. fingers to shape into a round. If using square wrappers, dip your finger in water, and gently press the corners down so it looks like a little basket.
8. Push a pea into the top of each Siu Mai
9. Line a 30cm/12" bamboo steamer (or stove steamer) with a steamer liner (or a piece of baking paper with holes in it).
10. Fill a wok big enough to hold your steamer with about 2 cups of water. Bring to rapid simmer over medium high heat.
11. Place Siu Mai in steamer. Put the lid on, place the steamer on the wok over simmering water. Steam 10 minutes, or
12. until internal temperature of dumplings is 75°C/165°F and it's cooked through.
13. Serve immediately with dipping sauce!

NOTES Usually this would be made with pork mince, but as Elly doesn't eat pork, I've altered this recipe slightly. <3

Makes 24 pieces

45 minutes

Recipe contributed from Singapore

INGREDIENTS

3 dried shiitake mushrooms

350g/13oz chicken mince

¾ teaspoon salt

2½ teaspoons sugar

1 teaspoon light soy sauce

1½ teaspoons Chinese cooking wine (aka Shaoxing wine)

150g/5oz precooked prawns/shrimp

2 tablespoons white part of spring/green onions, finely minced

20 - 25 wonton wrappers/egg wrappers 8cm/3.5" squares/rounds

Handful of peas

Soy sauce

Chinese black or white vinegar

Chinese chilli paste (or Sriracha)

YORKSHIRE PUDDING

SIDE

DIRECTIONS

1. Combine eggs, flour, milk, water, and salt in a medium bowl and whisk until a smooth batter is formed.
2. Let batter rest at room temperature for at least 30 minutes.
3. Alternatively, for best results, transfer to an airtight container and refrigerate batter overnight or for up to 3 days. Remove from refrigerator while you preheat the oven, and allow it to return to room temperature.
4. Adjust oven rack to centre position and preheat oven to 230°C /450°F.
5. Divide the goose fat/oil evenly between 2 popover pans (or a 12-well standard muffin tin or a 24-well mini muffin tin).
6. Preheat in the oven until the fat is smoking hot, about 10 minutes.
7. Transfer the pans/ tins to a heat-proof surface (such as an aluminium baking sheet on your stovetop), and divide the batter evenly between every well between ½ - ¾ full.
8. Immediately return to oven. Bake until the yorkshire puddings have just about quadrupled in volume, are deep brown all over, crisp to the touch, and sound hollow when tapped, about 15 minutes.
9. Serve immediately, before they have a chance to get cold.

Makes 12

30 minutes + resting time

Recipe contributed from Yorkshire, England

INGREDIENTS

4 large eggs

150g/5.25oz all-purpose flour

¾ cup whole milk

½ teaspoon kosher salt

1 tablespoon + 2 teaspoons water

100ml/ ½ cup goose fat/vegetable oil

NOTES

Can't have a British roast without Yorkshire Puddings. The single most important thing you can do is rest the batter. If you must, you can skip it, but your yorkies will be significantly worse for it. If using skim or low-fat milk, skip the water and increase amount of milk to 1 cup minus 2 tablespoons. If you have time, allow your batter to return to room temperature. The warmer your batter is to start, the better your puddings will rise. Warmer batter will create taller, crisper puddings with a more hollow core, more delicious to eat. Colder batter will create denser puddings with a more distinct cup (ideal for holding gravy).

EASY MARMITE ROASTIES

SIDE

DIRECTIONS

1. Preheat oven to 190°C /375°F.
2. Add oil to a deep baking tray and put into the oven to heat up whilst you prepare the potatoes.
3. Heat a pan of water on the hob.
4. Peel potatoes and chop to desired size (not too small).
5. Pop them in the boiling water and parboil for 10 minutes, just until the edges of the potatoes start to get soft.
6. Drain the potatoes, and in the same pan replace the lid and give them a really good shake until the edges start to fluff up.
7. Add a small drizzle of oil, marmite and salt/pepper seasoning.
8. Replace lid and shake, coating the potatoes evenly.
9. Take the baking tray out of the oven and carefully tip the potatoes in the tray. Careful of spitting oil!
10. Make sure the potatoes are evenly spread in the tray.
11. Place in the oven on the middle shelf for 30 minutes, turning regularly.
12. Remove from the oven and enjoy (they are amazing with gravy!)

Serves 4

50 minutes

Recipe contributed from the UK

INGREDIENTS

4 medium/large white potatoes

4 tablespoons cooking oil (my favourite is rapeseed)

1 tablespoon marmite

Salt and pepper for seasoning

ABOUT

Contributed by Eleni's family. Eleni is 3 years old and has severe NKH. We all know what devastation this condition puts upon our children and their families. Hopefully, with this cookbook, it will raise not only funds to help find a cure for NKH, but also bring awareness to the condition too. Thank you to everyone who has provided recipes and has shown support. You can find out more about Eleni at facebook.com/elenisusanshaw

DUCHESS POTATOES

SIDE

DIRECTIONS

1. Line a baking sheet with parchment paper.
2. In a large pot, cover potatoes with water and bring to a boil. Reduce to a simmer and cook until potatoes are soft, approximately 20 to 25 minutes.
3. Drain then return potatoes to the pot. Pass potatoes through potato mill or ricer into a large bowl (or mash).
4. Add 4 tablespoons cream, butter, and ¾ teaspoon each salt and pepper to potatoes. Adjust seasoning to taste and add remaining 1 tablespoon cream to get a pipeable consistency, if necessary.
5. Cool potatoes 5 minutes, then fold 1 egg yolk at a time with a flexible spatula until incorporated.
6. Fit a pastry bag with a large star tip and transfer the potatoes to the piping bag. Pipe crowns with a 3" base, swirling into a point. Refrigerate for 1 hour, if possible.
7. 30 minutes before baking, preheat oven to 200°C/400°C.
8. Bake potatoes for 10 minutes, then reduce temperature to 190°C/375°F. Bake 8 to 12 minutes more, until golden brown.
9. Serve hot, sprinkled with parsley and flaky sea salt, if you like.

Serves 8

90 minutes +
60 minutes chilling

Recipe contributed
from the UK

INGREDIENTS

900g/2lbs Yukon Gold potatoes, peeled and quartered

4 tablespoons heavy cream

4 tablespoons butter

Kosher salt

Freshly ground black pepper

2 large egg yolks

Finely chopped fresh parsley leaves, for garnish

Flaky sea salt, for garnish

NOTES

Duchess Potatoes is a classic French dish, that looks SUPER fancy. It's all in the shape, with the potato piped through a star tip. If you don't have one, use a ziplock bag and cut off a corner to pipe the crowns. To create uniform shapes, stencil 3" circles on the parchment paper, then flip over to pipe. If you want to get fancy with the flavouring, add in minced roasted garlic and parmesan - delicious!

POTATO CASSEROLE

SIDE

Serves 8-10

90 minutes

Recipe ("famous" in Utah) contributed from the USA
- Thanks Klark! :)

DIRECTIONS

1. Preheat oven to 180°C/350°F.
2. In a medium sized skillet, add 2 tablespoons butter and the onions, sauté until the onions are translucent. Add the garlic and cook until fragrant. Remove from heat and set aside.
3. In a large bowl, mix together the cooked onions, garlic, hash browns, condensed soup, sour cream, parmesan cheese, salt, pepper, and 1 ½ cups cheddar cheese.
4. Spread into a 9x13 inch baking pan. Top with remaining ½ cup cheddar cheese.
5. Melt the remaining 4 tablespoons of butter and mix with the crushed cornflake crumbs. Sprinkle evenly over the top of the casserole.
6. Bake for 50-60 minutes or until cooked throughout and bubbly. Serve!

INGREDIENTS

6 tablespoons butter

¾ cup onion, diced

2 cloves garlic, minced

30oz/850g bag of frozen, shredded hash brown potatoes, thawed -or- 12 small potatoes parboiled and shredded

10.5oz/296g can condensed cream of chicken soup

1 cup sour cream or plain greek yogurt

¼ cup grated parmesan cheese

1 teaspoon salt

½ teaspoon ground pepper

2 cups sharp cheddar cheese shredded and firmly packed

1½ cups crushed cornflake cereal or panko bread crumbs

MINI ROASTED CARROTS

SIDE

DIRECTIONS

1. Preheat oven to 230°C/450°F.
2. Place the carrots and garlic in a greased 15x10 inch pan.
3. Drizzle with oil and vinegar.
4. Sprinkle with the thyme, salt and pepper; gently toss to coat.
5. Cover and bake 20 minutes, then stir.
6. Bake, uncovered, 10 minutes, then stir again.
7. Bake until carrots are crisp tender, 10 minutes longer.
8. If desired, sprinkle with fresh thyme, and serve!

NOTES

For a little heat, try adding ½ teaspoon chilli powder and a dash of cayenne pepper. If you don't have baby carrots on hand, use medium carrots; cut them into 2 inch pieces and roast for 25 minutes.

Serves 8

50 minutes

Recipe contributed from the USA

INGREDIENTS

900g/2lbs baby carrots

6 garlic cloves, peeled

2 tablespoons olive oil

2 teaspoons white wine vinegar

1-2 teaspoons dried thyme

½ teaspoon salt

⅛ teaspoon pepper

Fresh thyme, optional

BAKED PUMPKIN AND BRIE
SIDE

DIRECTIONS

1. Preheat oven to 220°C/430°F.
2. Peel, remove the seeds and slice your pumpkins into 5mm slices.
3. Heat olive oil in a medium saucepan over medium-high heat. Add the onion, garlic, sugar and thyme.
4. Stir frequently for 5-6 minutes or until onions begin to caramelise.
5. Stir in the passata and bring to the boil.
6. Stir in the parsley.
7. Reduce heat to low and simmer for 5 minutes.
8. Remove from the heat and gradually whisk in the butter.
9. Season to taste.
10. Spoon one-third of the sauce over the base of a 3L-capacity ovenproof dish.
11. Layer pumpkin over the sauce, then spoon over remaining sauce.
12. Scatter with the cheeses.
13. Cover with baking paper then foil.
14. Bake for 1 hour, remove foil and baking paper and bake for 20-25 minutes until pumpkin is cooked.
15. Sprinkle over pumpkin seeds and extra thyme leaves.
16. Stand for 15 minutes before serving.

Serves 8

90 minutes

Recipe contributed from France

INGREDIENTS

80ml/ ⅓ cup extra virgin olive oil

1 large brown onion, sliced into rings

4 garlic cloves, crushed

2 tablespoons brown sugar

¼ bunch thyme, leaves picked

2 x 750ml jar tomato passata

¼ bunch curly parsley, leaves picked, finely chopped

80g unsalted butter, roughly chopped

2 large butternut pumpkins (1kg each)

250g roughly chopped brie

250g comté cheese, finely grated

40g/¼ cup toasted pumpkin/pepita seeds

BABA'S WARM POTATO SALAD

SIDE

DIRECTIONS

1. Peel your potatoes and cut into half-inch pieces.
2. In salted water, boil potatoes until soft (but firmer than if you were going to mash them).
3. In the meantime, cut the carrots and celery into small chunks.
4. Drain the potatoes and move to large bowl (this potato salad is only good when it's still warm, so don't let them cool).
5. Season with salt, pepper and garlic powder.
6. Add veg oil, mayo, carrots and celery and stir to combine.
7. Add half of the apple cider/vinegar, stir and taste.
8. Continue adding vinegar until it's right for you - my family likes it very vinegary.
9. Serve immediately and enjoy!

Serves 4-6

25 minutes

Recipe contributed from Buffalo, NY

INGREDIENTS

900g/2lbs potatoes

2 carrots

2 pieces of celery

1 tablespoon veg oil (any kind)

½ cup mayonnaise

⅓ cup apple cider or white vinegar (or to taste)

Salt, pepper, garlic powder to taste

ABOUT

This is a family recipe passed down four generations. It originally came from Kiev, Ukraine, where my Bubbie was raised. Goes great with crispy baked chicken wings as a homage to where my Baba lived most of her life, Buffalo New York. Recipe contributed by Katie Sidell-Schneider, who used to work with Sam at #Bazaarvoice #dontStopBelieving

SCALLOPED CORN CASSEROLE

SIDE

Serves 6

45 minutes

Recipe contributed from Colorado, USA

DIRECTIONS

1. Preheat oven to 180°C /350°F.
2. In bowl combine all ingredients.
3. Pour into greased casserole dish.
4. Bake, uncovered, for 40 minutes or until slightly brown.
5. Serve!

INGREDIENTS

425g/15oz can cream corn

425g/15oz can whole kernel corn

240g/8½oz box corn muffin mix

1 cup sour cream

3 eggs, slightly beaten

½ cup melted butter

ABOUT

Recipe submitted by Kris on behalf of The Skinner Family. She says "Handed down from my husband's grandmother."

KETO CREAMED SPINACH

SIDE

Serves 3

15 minutes

Recipe contributed from Aoteroa/New Zealand

DIRECTIONS

1. Defrost frozen spinach in the microwave (around 6-7 minutes).
2. Heat a pan on the stove to medium-high heat. Once the pan is hot, add the spinach and wait for the water to boil off.
3. Season the spinach and mix.
4. Add cream cheese and stir til melted.
5. Add sour cream and mix. Turn down the heat to low.
6. Add parmesan cheese and stir until the creamed spinach thickens.
7. Serve!

INGREDIENTS

285g/10oz frozen spinach

3 tablespoons parmesan cheese

85g/3oz cream cheese

2 tablespoons sour cream

¼ teaspoon garlic powder

¼ teaspoon onion powder

Salt and pepper to taste

NOTES

Each serving comes out to be 165 Calories, 13.22g Fats, 3.63g Net Carbs, and 7.33g Protein.

ONE POT TEX MEX RICE

SIDE

Serves 6

20 minutes

Recipe contributed from the USA

INGREDIENTS

3 cups quick-cooking rice (also known as easy cook rice)

2 tablespoons taco seasoning

3 ½ cups chicken broth

395g/14oz can diced tomatoes with chillies, drained

½ cup red bell pepper, diced

½ cup red onion, diced

3 cloves garlic, minced

½ cup canned black beans (washed and drained)

½ cup frozen corn

½ teaspoon salt

½ teaspoon black pepper

2 tablespoons olive oil

½ cup Colby Jack cheese, shredded

½ cup Monterey Jack cheese, shredded

½ cup coriander/cilantro, chopped

DIRECTIONS

1. Dice the red pepper, and onions into a large pot or dutch oven. Add the minced garlic.
2. Drain the canned tomatoes and wash and drain the black beans, and add to the pot.
3. Add the rest of the ingredients except the cheese and coriander/cilantro.
4. Stir to combine and bring to a boil.
5. Cover, and cook for 10-12 minutes or until liquid is absorbed and rice is cooked.
6. Stir in cheese and sprinkle with coriander/cilantro and the spring/green onions.
7. Serve immediately.

NOTES

Taco seasoning: into a small bowl, add ¼ teaspoon of cayenne, ½ teaspoons of oregano, garlic powder, pepper and onion powder, 1 ½ teaspoons of paprika and cumin, 2 teaspoons of salt and 1 tablespoon of chilli powder. For those outside the US, Gouda is a good Monterey Jack alternative. For Colby Jack, a mild, unaged cheddar.

SPICY AND SMOKEY BEANS

SIDE

DIRECTIONS

1. In a skillet or large pan, heat the olive oil on a low heat and add the pancetta.
2. Whilst the pancetta cooks, finely dice the onion and garlic, then add them to the pan with a splash of water and continue to cook on a low heat for 10 minutes, until the onion is soft.
3. Meanwhile, chop the peppers into small pieces and then add to the pan. Cook for a further ten minutes before adding the tomato purée, Worcestershire sauce, and tinned tomatoes.
4. Turn up the heat until the sauce starts to boil, then bring down to a low temperature and add the rest of the ingredients.
5. Cover with a lid and leave to cook for minimum half an hour. You can make this ahead of time and leave to cook on a low heat for as long as you like to help the flavours develop.
6. Once ready, season with salt and pepper and serve with chunks of crusty bread.

ABOUT

Recipe submitted and illustrated by Zoë Ellison. Since discovering smokey baked beans in a cafe in Bath many years ago, I have endeavoured to create my own recipe that balances the sweet and spicy elements perfectly and can be eaten any time of day.

Serves 8 (or 4 as a main)

60 minutes

Recipe contributed from the UK

INGREDIENTS

1 tablespoon of olive oil

1 pack of pancetta

1 large brown onion

2 cloves of garlic

2 peppers, yellow and orange

1 tablespoon tomato purée (in the UK, tomato paste in the US)

1 tin of chopped tomatoes

200ml beef stock

2 tins of cannellini beans (drained)

1 tablespoon Worcestershire sauce

1 tablespoon brown sugar

1 teaspoon chilli powder

1 teaspoon smoked paprika

1 teaspoon cumin

JAMAICAN RICE AND PEAS

SIDE

DIRECTIONS

1. Add the pimento berries, ginger, salt, coconut milk, water, thyme, scallion, onion, garlic, and scotch bonnet pepper to a pot to make a broth. Cover and bring to a boil.
2. Drain your beans and give them a good rinse.
3. Wash your rice until the water runs clear (4-5 times) and drain.
4. Add the rice and beans. Return the lid to the pot and return to a boil. Turn the heat to low and let the rice steam until all the water evaporates, about 20 minutes. Do not remove the lid.
5. Turn the heat off. Do not remove the lid, do not peek. Leave the rice covered, for another 5 minutes, undisturbed.
6. Fluff the rice, taste, and season if needed.
7. Remove the thyme stems and the scotch bonnet pepper.
8. Serve with a wedge of lime and a sprig of thyme.

Serves 4

35 minutes

Recipe contributed from the UK

INGREDIENTS

1 (400g/14oz) can red kidney beans

1 cup fresh coconut milk (or ½ cup canned coconut milk)

275g/1½ cup long grain white rice, washed and drained

1 red onion, chopped

4 cloves of garlic, crushed

2 spring onions/scallions, chopped

8 sprigs of thyme

1 scotch bonnet pepper (don't cut or burst)

5 pimento berries (allspice)

2 teaspoons salt

a thumb of ginger

750ml/3 cups water

lime wedges

ABOUT

In Jamaica, dried beans are known as peas, which is why some people call this dish rice and peas and others know it as beans and rice. Most people make the dish with either pigeon peas (known as gungo peas in Jamaica) or dried kidney beans.

TOMATO CHEDDAR RICE

SIDE

DIRECTIONS

1. Rinse basmati rice very well before cooking. Wash 4 to 5 times until the water runs clear. This will help remove starch from the surface of the grains, which will help with fluffy rice! Do not skip this step, it is crucial that you rinse the rice however many times it takes for the water to run clear.
2. To a pot, add the minced garlic, chilli and chopped onion with a little oil, and heat until the onion is tender and the garlic fragrant, around 5-7 minutes.
3. Add the salt and tomatoes, using the back of a wooden spoon to lightly crush them. Add chicken stock and bring to a boil.
4. Add the washed rice, pop on the pot lid and turn the heat down low. Do not remove the lid for 20 minutes or so. During this time the rice will cook and absorb all the liquid.
5. Preheat oven to 260°C /500°F (don't skip this step)
6. After 20 minutes, turn the heat off but leave the rice covered and undisturbed for 5 more minutes.
7. Give the rice mix a good stir, and transfer to an oven-proof dish. Add the cheese in a layer on top.
8. Switch the now-hot oven to broil and place the baking dish on the oven rack closest to the broiler. Broil until the top bubbles and turns golden brown and crispy, about 10-15 minutes.
9. Serve immediately.

ABOUT

Basically, pizza in rice form. It's proper good. It's flexible, add in grilled chicken or chorizo. I once cracked four eggs on the top and left it a bit longer in the oven. Yum!

Serves 4

45 minutes

Recipe contributed from the UK

INGREDIENTS

2 tablespoons olive oil

3 cloves of garlic, minced

1 small yellow onion, chopped

1 small chilli, finely chopped

10 plum tomatoes, or a can of whole or diced tomatoes (800g/28oz), strained

1 ½ teaspoon salt

1 cup basmati rice

1 ½ cups of chicken broth

3 cups shredded sharp cheddar cheese

VEGAN PESTO

SIDE

240 minutes soaking and 15 minutes blending.

Recipe contributed from Melbourne, VIC, Australia

INGREDIENTS

250g cashews

200m extra virigin olive oil

1-2 bunches of basil

1-2 cloves of garlic

salt and pepper to taste

DIRECTIONS

1. Soak cashews in filtered water for at least 4 hours
2. Place all ingredients in a blender and blend until smooth, add water until desired consistency is achieved.

NOTES

Adapted pesto recipes for allergies! Activated (soaked) cashews are a great base for creamy goodness. Refrigerate for up to 3 days. Use as a dip for pesto chicken pasta or zucchini spaghetti, make it creamy with nut milk of choice.

RED ONION MARMALADE

SIDE

35 minutes

Recipe contributed from Aoteroa/New Zealand

INGREDIENTS

1 tablespoon oil

1 tablespoon mustard seeds

1 tablespoon sweet chilli sauce

1 large red onion, finely chopped

50g brown sugar

125ml red wine

75ml balsamic vinegar

DIRECTIONS

1. Heat 1 tablespoon oil in a pan, add 3 large, finely sliced red onions and 1 tablespoon of mustard seeds and cook for 5 minutes.
2. Add 50g brown sugar, 1 tablespoon sweet chilli sauce and 75ml cold water. Cover and cook for 15 minutes, then add 125ml red wine and 75ml balsamic vinegar.
3. Bring to a boil and simmer for 15-20 minutes until syrupy, then serve.

HOT HONEY SAUCE

SIDE

45 minutes

Recipe contributed from Sweden

INGREDIENTS

339g/1 cup honey

1 teaspoon chilli flakes

½ teaspoon cayenne pepper

½ teaspoon brown sugar

⅛ teaspoon salt

DIRECTIONS

1. Add all the ingredients to a heavy-bottom saucepan.
2. Heat over medium until the honey is quite hot.
3. Turn off the heat and allow to infuse for 30 minutes.
4. Pour into a squeeze bottle and use as desired.

NOTES

Well good. For milder sauce, strain the chilli flakes or add more honey. We like it on pizza, or as a dipping sauce for chicken nuggets or grilled cheese sandwiches. I've used it as a glaze on salmon, but it is ESPECIALLY good with a cheese board. My kid likes it on french toast (especially when served with bacon and fried chicken!) Keep at room temperature for 6+ months in an airtight container.

EASY HOLLANDAISE SAUCE

SIDE

5 minutes

Recipe contributed from Aoteroa/New Zealand

INGREDIENTS

2 large egg yolks

¼ medium lemon, juiced, or to taste

1 pinch salt

1 pinch cayenne pepper

¼ cup salted butter, melted

DIRECTIONS

1. Beat egg yolks, lemon juice, salt, and cayenne pepper together in a microwave-safe bowl until smooth.
2. Mix in the mayo.
3. Slowly stream melted butter into the egg yolk mixture while whisking to incorporate.
4. Heat sauce in the microwave on medium for 15 to 20 seconds; whisk until well combined.
5. If the sauce separates after microwaving, add a splash of water and whisk until combined

NOTES

If you're not a fan of lemon, use half the recommended amount, and if you feel like it should be creamier, you can add a tablespoon of mayo after you beat the yolks but before the butter. It's unexpectedly good!

DESSERTS

BOBBIE BLUE'S FAMOUS FUDGE

DESSERT

DIRECTIONS

1. Grease a 10-inch square tin with olive oil.
2. Scrape the condensed milk into a good-sized, thick pan.
3. Measure the water into the tin, swill, then add to pan.
4. Dice the butter and add with the sugar, syrup and salt to the pan.
5. Heat over a low heat till the sugar has dissolved and there is no grittiness on bottom of pan. This stage takes some time. Stir occasionally with a wooden spoon, keep the heat low.
6. When sugar has completely dissolved, raise the heat and boil the resultant fudge fairly fast, stirring constantly, ensuring the spoon gets into the angle between the side and base of pan.
7. When the fudge has become darker and thicker test by dropping a little into a basin of cold water. Scoop it out and test its consistency between finger and thumb. When it forms a soft ball that holds its shape, the fudge is ready.
   If in doubt boil the fudge for a little longer.
8. When satisfied, take it off the heat, and allow it too cool slightly.
9. Add a small teaspoon of vanilla essence and beat vigorously until the mixture begins to get stiff.
10. Pour it quickly into the prepared tin and leave til it hardens.
11. Score into squares, leave to harden further before cutting. Store in an air-tight tin.

Makes approximately 36 squares

55 minutes

Recipe contributed from the UK

INGREDIENTS

550g/1 ¼ lb granulated sugar

150g/5oz butter or margarine

1 400g can full cream condensed milk

8 tablespoons Warm water (measure carefully)

3 rounded dessert spoons of Golden Syrup

a good pinch of salt

Vanilla essence flavouring (optional)

ABOUT

Recipe contributed by Sam, Mikaere's Dad: "My grandmother would make this fudge as a treat, it's the best fudge I've ever had! Likely taken from one of her mother's recipe books so it's probably 80+ years old... I now use a cooking thermometer to make sure I get the fudge to the right temperature, you want to get it to 115 °C. Get ready for an arm workout because to get the best crumbly fudge you'll want to vigorously beat it as hard as you can. I usually go until the spoon stands up in the mixture."

PEANUTBUTTER NO BAKES

DESSERT

DIRECTIONS

1. Melt butter over high heat.
2. Add milk and sugar.
3. Once it comes to an uncontrollable boil, cook for 3 minutes.
4. Remove from the heat and add vanilla, peanut butter, oats and chocolate chips and mix well.
5. Drop onto wax paper, and flatten with a spoon.
6. Allow to cool for about 45-60 minutes or until the cookies have firmed up, serve, and enjoy!

ABOUT

This is one of our favorite family cookies we love to share. Submitted by Tanya Graves, who says: "Ezmerae is a very beautiful eleven month old girl who has NKH. She is our family Gem. We have overcome so many things and still many more things to achieve."

Makes 24

30 minutes

Recipe contributed from the USA

INGREDIENTS

6 cups oats

225g/2 sticks of butter

1 cup milk

3 cups sugar

1 cup peanut butter

1 teaspoon vanilla

handful of chocolate chips

ELLY'S CHOCOLATE CHIP COOKIES

DESSERT

DIRECTIONS

1. Preheat your oven to 190°C/375°F.
2. Cream butter and sugar till very very light coloured + fluffy (cream for approximately 5 minutes, at least).
3. Gradually add the beaten egg, and mix well.
4. Sift in the flour and salt, and mix well.
5. Stir in the chocolate chips.
6. Use a tablespoon to scoop out a small amount of dough (maybe half a teaspoon at a time), and roll it into a ball.
7. Place on a metal baking tray, lined with baking paper.
8. Once your tray is full, use a fork to slightly squish your cookies.
9. Bake for 10-12 minutes, until the bottoms are golden brown.

Makes 12-15

30 minutes

Recipe contributed from the UK

INGREDIENTS

125g softened butter

125g brown sugar

pinch of salt

1 beaten egg

200g of self raising flour

125g of milk chocolate chips

NOTES

This is the perfect cookie and scales well. I've often gifted these and they've always gone down a treat. Make sure you use light brown, softened sugar. White sugar (or caster sugar) behaves differently than brown sugar, particularly with softened butter. Sugar can play a critical role in gluten development by acting as a tenderiser, but white sugar, with its neutral pH, interferes with gluten development, allowing the dough to spread more before it sets. Acidic brown sugar, on the other hand, speeds gluten formation and egg protein coagulation, so the dough sets quickly, making cookies thick and tender/chewy. It's a whole thing. Make sure you use a metal baking tray, rather than a glass or a silicone mat, though aluminium is better than stainless steel for conducting heat and baking foods evenly. Also, it's better to bake one tray at a time, pulling one out of the oven and sliding the next one in, as it means the cookies evenly cook from two heat sources. While you can bake two trays at a time, since the heat in the oven comes from only one source, areas of the oven, they may cook unevenly. When baking two sheets at a time, you should rotate them -- both front to back and switching shelves -- halfway through the baking time. Yeah, baking with a chemistry and physics lens. it makes better cookies.

FLAPJACKS

DESSERT

Makes 16

30 minutes

Recipe contributed from the UK

DIRECTIONS

1. Preheat the oven to 160°C/320°F.
2. Melt butter, sugar and golden syrup together.
3. Once melted add the oats, add up to 50g extra if it is too gooey.
4. Tip into a lined (greaseproof paper or silicone liner) tin, press down very firmly, and bake for 20mins.
6. Wait until it is cold to slice it.

INGREDIENTS

150g butter

150g demerara sugar

4 tablespoons golden syrup

300g porridge oats

NOTES

Very easy to double the recipe for events, very easy to make and well delicious! Submitted by Jessica Ashbridge - thank you so much! :)

CAN I HAVE THAT RECIPE - ROCKY ROAD

DESSERT

DIRECTIONS

1. Melt the butter, broken-up chocolate and golden syrup gently in a large saucepan.
2. Put the biscuits in a freezer bag and bash with a rolling pin until you have a mixture of crumbs and chunks.
3. Add the biscuits to the chocolate mix and stir to coat. Add the other ingredients and stir again.
4. Tip into a lightly greased foil shallow tray or Tupperware tray and flatten with a spatula.
5. Refrigerate for a minimum of 2 hours.
6. Tip onto a chopping board and cut into chunks. Sieve a small amount of icing sugar or cocoa over the bars.

Makes 24 slices

120 minutes

Recipe contributed from the UK

INGREDIENTS

125g soft butter

300g chocolate (milk or plain but decent quality)

3 x 15ml tablespoons golden syrup

200g Rich Tea biscuits

100g dried cherries or cranberries

100g Smarties, chopped Brazil nuts, mini marshmallows or anything else that takes your fancy

Icing sugar or cocoa for dusting

ABOUT

Recipe submitted by The Makepeace family. Our beautiful daughter Georgia was born in 2003 with NKH. Despite having to negotiate her own rocky road when she was born, she lived a happy life until we lost her at 12. She loved being part of family life with her younger brother and would happily help finish off the chocolatey residue from the mixing bowl.

LEMON BARS

DESSERT

DIRECTIONS

1. Preheat oven to 180 °C/350 °F.
2. In a bowl, mix softened butter, 2 cups flour and ½ cup sugar.
3. Press into the bottom of an 8x11 inch greased pan.
4. Bake for 15 - 20 minutes in the preheated oven, or until slightly golden. Allow to cool.
5. In another bowl whisk the remaining 1½ cups sugar, ⅓ cup of flour and lemon zest.
6. Whisk in the eggs and lemon juice.
7. Pour over the baked crust (make sure the crust is cool).
8. Bake for an additional 25 minutes in the preheated oven.
9. Allow the bars to cool slightly (warm, but not hot) and dust with icing sugar.
10. The bars will firm up as they cool. Cool completely before cutting and serving. Store in fridge.

Serves 4

35 minutes

Recipe contributed from Spain

INGREDIENTS

BASE

225g/1 cup butter, softened

100g/½ cup white sugar

246g/2 cups all-purpose flour

2 eggs

LEMON TOPPING

250g/1½ cups white sugar

40g/⅓ cup all-purpose flour

⅔ cup juice from just juiced lemons (approx 3 large lemons)

Zest from 2 lemons

¼ teaspoon salt

Icing sugar

NOTES

These bars also work well with limes. If you have the time, instead of dusting with icing sugar, make a lemon glaze: mix 100g/1 cup of icing sugar mixed with 40ml/ 2½ tablespoons of freshly squeezed lemon juice (the juice from one lemon). You can add two drops of yellow food colouring if you prefer the yellow aesthetic. Pour the glaze over when it comes out of the oven, and allow to cool in the pan.

LOLLY CAKE (KIWI CLASSIC!)

DESSERT

DIRECTIONS

1. In a ziplock bag, crush the malt biscuits until you have a variety of chunks, some crumbs, some large and some small pieces.
2. Cut the explorer lollies into bite-sized chunks and add to the biscuits.
3. In a saucepan, warm the butter and condensed milk.
4. Add the biscuit pieces and the lollies to the butter and condensed milk mix, and stir to combine.
5. Tip out onto a chopping board, and use your hands to form a firm log shape (the heat of your hands is key to getting a good texture).
6. Roll/pat the log in coconut, till it's covered.
7. Chill in the fridge for up to 4 hours.
8. When set, cut into slices and serve. Sweet as!

Makes 12 slices

20 minutes + chill time

Recipe contributed from New Zealand

INGREDIENTS

250g malt biscuits/graham crackers

190g Explorer lollies (previously known as Eskimos, a type of firm marshmallow)

120g butter

200g/½ a tin of sweetened condensed milk

desiccated coconut

ABOUT

This is a very kiwi recipe. Do not make the mistake of substituting the explorer lollies/sweets with regular/soft marshmallows. In a pinch, foam sweets (like foam bananas or shrimp over regular/soft marshmallows) might work.

RUM BALLS

DESSERT

DIRECTIONS

1. In a food processor, pulse biscuits until fine crumbs.
2. Add crumbs to a large bowl with the condensed milk, coconut, sifted cocoa and rum. Stir well to combine.
3. Roll mixture into walnut-sized balls.
4. Toss balls in chocolate sprinkles, desiccated coconut, icing sugar or crushed candied nuts.
5. Place on a tray; cover, and refrigerate until firm.

ABOUT

A very Christmas-esque treat! DId you know Rum Balls were originally invented by the Danish bakers, who made them from yesterday's unsold cakes. They called them "Romkugler". These ones are especially good, and wonderful for gifting.

Makes 30

20 minutes

Recipe contributed from the UK

INGREDIENTS

250g plain biscuits (such as Nilla Wafers, or malt biscuits)

395g can sweetened condensed milk

80g/1 cup desiccated coconut

25g/¼ cup cocoa powder

60ml/¼ cup dark rum

chocolate sprinkles, desiccated coconut, cocoa powder, icing sugar or candied nuts for coating.

EASY ENERGY BALLS

DESSERT

DIRECTIONS

1. Add all ingredients into a large mixing bowl and stir everything together until combined.
2. If it's too wet, add more oats, if too dry add more peanut butter. You're aiming for a stickyish dough that holds together when rolled into a ball.
3. Chill the mixture in the bowl in the refrigerator for a few hours, this will help the mixture stick together more easily.
4. Roll into balls. Roll into mixture into 1-inch balls.
5. Eat immediately.

NOTES

The best kind of peanut butter to use will be a thick creamy kind, not runny and oily. This is important to ensure everything binds well together. If you have trouble getting the energy balls to hold together, I recommend adding in more peanut butter to make the mixture a bit more sticky Add other ingredients too, peanuts work a treat, raisins, or a tablespoon or two of protein powder.

Makes 18

40 minutes

Recipe contributed from the UK

INGREDIENTS

1 cup whole oats

2 dessert spoons chia seeds

2 dessert spoons flaxseed

125g peanut butter

90g honey or maple syrup

½ teaspoon salt

100g chocolate chips

Pinch of salt

BANANA POPS

DESSERT

DIRECTIONS

1. Peel and break bananas in half.
2. Insert a wooden stick into each banana piece. Arrange bananas on a parchment-lined baking sheet and freeze until firm, 2 hours.
3. In a medium microwave-safe bowl, heat chocolate chips in 10-second increments, stirring between each, until melted and smooth.
4. Working quickly, dip each banana piece in chocolate, shake off excess, and cover with sprinkles.
5. Chocolate should set quickly, but if necessary, freeze pops to harden the coating before serving.

Makes 16

10 minutes

Recipe contributed from Canada

INGREDIENTS

4-5 firm-ripe bananas

1 cup/6oz semisweet chocolate chips

1 tablespoon sprinkles

BANANA BUTTER BITES

DESSERT

DIRECTIONS

1. Peel and slice bananas into rounds.
2. Spread a half teaspoon of peanut butter on each slice.
3. Sprinkle with chocolate chips and sprinkles.
4. Spear with a mini popsicle stick, and serve!

Makes 8 slices per banana

5 minutes

Recipe contributed from the USA

INGREDIENTS

Peanut Butter

Firm just ripe banana

Mini chocolate chips

Sprinkles

Mini popsicle sticks

FROZEN STRAWBERRY BARK

DESSERT

DIRECTIONS

1. In a freezer-safe tin, line with parchment.
2. Spread the yoghurt along the bottom, maybe 1cm thick.
3. Sprinkle with the strawberries and any other mix-ins.
4. Freeze for at least 6 hours, till completely frozen.
5. Remove from the pan, break into pieces, and serve!

Makes 8 slices per banana

5 minutes + 6 hours freezing time

Recipe contributed from the USA

INGREDIENTS

Greek Yoghurt

Freeze-dried strawberries

Anything else you'd like to mix in (cereal, fruit, nuts, sprinkles, chocolate chips, coconut, pretzels etc)

MUM'S PAV

DESSERT

DIRECTIONS

1. Put everything into the mixer and beat until smooth and shiny. Extra water can be added if needed, but do so in small amounts and carefully.
2. Bake at 180°C/355°F for 10 mins. Reduce heat to 150°C/300°F and bake a further 45 minutes or longer if required. DO NOT open the oven, allow to cool.
4. Once cool, decorate with whipped cream (I add a touch of vanilla essence to the cream) and fresh fruit.
6. Crumb a flake or chocolate over top.

NOTES

Submitted by Liz Horne, in honour of her Mum, Anne. Adapted from an Edmund's cookbook recipe. Place on baking tray lined with paper. Don't spread too thin. Quantities in brackets are for a larger Pavlova. DO NOT open the oven during cooking time otherwise you risk collapsing the pav. Check regularly and gauge when the meringue is crisp on the outside. Turn the oven off and allow to cool. The heat will continue to cook the pav for a period thereafter.

Serves 6 (or 12 with bracketed quantities)

70 minutes

Recipe contributed from Aoteroa/New Zealand

INGREDIENTS

2 (or 4) egg whites

1½ (or 3) **cups** icing sugar

1 (or 2) **teaspoons** cornflour

1 (or 2) **teaspoons** vinegar

½ (or 1) **teaspoons** vanilla essence

¼ (or ½) **cup** boiling water

Whipped cream for topping

Dash of vanilla essence

Fresh fruit to decorate

Flake or chocolate to crumb over top

SUNNY SIDE UP MERINGUES

DESSERT

DIRECTIONS

1. If going the easy route, whip your cream. Place each meringue nest on a plate, and spoon a generous dollop of bought lemon curd into the middle. Add a dollop of whipped cream, and serve!

1. If making from scratch, for the meringues: preheat oven to 100 °C/225 °F. Place a single rack in the middle of the oven. Line large baking sheet with parchment paper.
2. In a bowl with mixer on medium, beat 3 egg whites with a pinch of salt until foamy. Add cream of tartar and beat on medium-high until soft peaks form. Add sugar 1 tablespoon at a time until peaks are stiff and glossy. Beat in vanilla.
3. Spoon meringue into piping bag fitted with star tip, or into resealable plastic bag with one corner cut off. Pipe six 3-inch disks onto baking sheet, spacing 1 inch apart. Pipe around edges of disks to form 3/4-inch-high sides. Bake 1 hour.
4. Turn oven off. Leave meringues in oven 1½ hours with oven door closed. Remove from oven; cool completely.
5. For the Tangy Lemon Curd: From 3 medium lemons, grate 1 tablespoon zest and squeeze 2/3 cups juice.
6. In heavy 2-quart saucepan on medium, heat sugar, butter, cornstarch, ¼ teaspoon salt, lemon juice and lemon zest to boiling. Boil 1 minute.
7. In small bowl, lightly beat 5 large egg yolks. Into yolks, beat small amount of lemon mixture. Off heat, whisk egg mixture back into lemon mixture in saucepan. Return to medium-low heat; cook stirring constantly, until thickened, about 5 minutes.
8. Pour lemon curd into bowl; cover surface area with plastic wrap and refrigerate 3+ hours.
9. To assemble, place each meringue nest on a plate, and spoon a generous dollop of lemon curd into the middle. Add a dollop of whipped cream, and serve!

Serves 6

10 minutes or 3 hours

Recipe contributed from the UK

INGREDIENTS

EASY

1 pack of meringue nests

1 jar of lemon curd (**¾ cup)**

1 carton double/heavy cream

FROM SCRATCH

MERINGUES

3 large egg whites

¼ teaspoon cream of tartar

½ cup sugar

½ teaspoon vanilla extract

LEMON CURD

3 medium lemons

1 cup sugar

6 tablespoons butter, cut up

1 tablespoons cornstarch

5 large egg yolks

1 carton double/heavy cream

VANILLA ROAST PEACHES

DESSERT

DIRECTIONS

1. Preheat oven to 200 °C/400 °F.
2. In a large, shallow baking dish, combine butter, lemon juice, sugar, and vanilla bean (seeds and pod).
3. Add peaches, and turn to coat with butter mixture; arrange, cut side down, in a single layer.
4. Roast until peaches are tender and cooking liquid is syrupy, 15 - 25 minutes, brushing with cooking liquid halfway through.
5. Fish out the bean pod.
6. Serve peaches (warm or at room temperature) with ice cream and raspberries; drizzle with cooking liquid.

NOTES

Very easy to make and well delicious. Don't skip the raspberries (they cut through the sweetness of the peaches/syrup). You can substitute the vanilla bean for 1 teaspoon of vanilla extract.

Serves 4

35 minutes

Recipe contributed from the USA

INGREDIENTS

2 tablespoons sugar

2 tablespoons unsalted butter, melted

2 tablespoons fresh lemon juice (from 1 lemon)

1 vanilla bean, halved lengthwise and scraped, to release the seeds

250g raspberries

4 firm, ripe peaches (500g - 750g), halved and pitted

vanilla ice cream, for serving

EASY MINI PAVS

DESSERT

DIRECTIONS

1. Dice your fruit into bite-sized pieces, and toss together.
2. Place each meringue nest in a bowl or a plate, and spoon a generous amount of the fruit salad into the middle.
3. Add several generous spoonfuls of whipped cream.
4. Top with berries, almonds and mint, and serve!

NOTES

Super easy, and looks so fancy. We like sprinkling chocolate flake over the top. Place a flake bar on a chopping board (in its wrapper) and hit gently with a rolling pin. Sprinkle over the top just before serving. Yum!

Serves 6

10 minutes

Recipe contributed from the UK

INGREDIENTS

6 meringue nests (bought or made)

1 carton double/heavy cream

Selection of fruit (Strawberries, blueberries, melon, peaches, kiwifruit, mango, apricot, plums, nectarines etc)

Almonds and mint for garnish

EASY OATY APPLE CRUMBLE

DESSERT

DIRECTIONS

1. Heat oven to fan 180C°C/355°F (skip if air frying).
2. Core and peel apples and roughly chop into thin slices.
3. Spread in the bottom of a small microwavable baking dish.
4. Sprinkle with sultanas or raisins and mix with apples.
5. Sprinkle over cinnamon to taste.
6. Add 1 tablespoon of maple syrup and give it all a good mix.
7. Cover and microwave for 3 mins. Mix again when cooked.
8. Put oats in a dish then in separate microwavable dish, put the butter and remaining 2 tablespoons of maple syrup.
9. Microwave until butter melts then mix with the oats.
10. Spread a layer of oats over the apples and bake in the top of an airfryer or fan oven at 180°C/355°F until the oats are golden and crunchy. Be careful, it's volcanic!
11. Serve with evaporated milk or custard.

Serves 3-4

15 minutes

Recipe contributed from Dorset, UK

INGREDIENTS

3 eating apples (like Royal Gala)

handful sultanas/raisins

3 tablespoons maple syrup

3 tablespoons butter

1½ cups porridge oats

ground cinnamon

evaporated milk or custard, for serving

NOTES

Contributed by The James-Hunt family. What's better on an Autumnal day in the UK, than the comfort of an apple crumble?

This quick and easy version is yummy and disappears so quickly in my family!! Inspired by the crumbles my Nanny used to make when I was a child.

THE CRUMBLE OF CRUMBLES

DESSERT

Serves 8

60 minutes

Recipe contributed from the UK

DIRECTIONS

1. Heat oven to 200°C/395°F (fan 180°C/355°F).
2. Peel, core and dice the fruit as appropriate, and place in an ovenproof dish.
3. Add 50g brown sugar, ginger and cinnamon and toss.
4. In a separate bowl, cut the cold butter into cubes, and add the flour.
5. With your fingers, rub the butter and flour until it resembles bread crumbs and there are no lumps.
6. Chop the almonds, and add to the topping, with the sugar and oats. Mix to combine.
7. Bake for 45 minutes until the topping is golden and the fruit is tender and juicy. Let rest for 5 minutes, then spoon into bowls.
8. Serve with ice cream or custard (or both!)

INGREDIENTS

Enough fruit to cover the bottom of your dish (we like a mix of pears, apples and berries, but also like peaches, nectarines, apricots, plums, rhubarb etc)

50g/1.8oz brown sugar

½ teaspoon ground ginger

½ teaspoon cinnamon

300g/10.5oz all-purpose flour

175g/6.2oz brown sugar

200g/7oz cold butter

½ cup oats

75g/2.6oz almonds

Custard or ice cream, to serve

VEGAN BROWNIE WITH RASPBERRIES + WALNUTS

DESSERT

DIRECTIONS

1. Preheat the oven to 180 °C/350 °F .
2. Line your brownie pan with baking paper/parchment. Do not skip this step.
3. In a large bowl, stir together the flour, sugar, cocoa powder, baking powder and salt.
4. Pour in water, vegetable oil and vanilla; mix until well blended.
5. Mix in the walnuts, saving a handful.
6. Spread evenly in a brownie pan.
7. Gently push your raspberries on the top till they are submerged in brownie.
8. Sprinkle the rest of your walnuts on top.
9. Bake for 30-40 minutes in the preheated oven, until the top is no longer shiny (or wobbly in the middle).
10. Let cool before cutting into squares.

Serves 4

Recipe contributed from the UK

INGREDIENTS

250g plain flour

300g demerara sugar

65g plain cocoa powder

1 teaspoon baking powder

1 teaspoon salt

250ml water

250ml vegetable oil

1 teaspoon salt

200g walnuts, chopped roughly

½ cup raspberries

ABOUT

This recipe is dedicated to the Sayin Family, and sweet baby Teo. They're new to the NKH community, but we're so glad to have met them!

RASPBERRY SOUFFLÉ

DESSERT

DIRECTIONS

RASPBERRY BASE

1. Dissolve the cornflour in a little cold water to form a smooth paste.
2. Bring the purée and sugar to the boil then add the cornflour.
3. Mix and simmer for a few minutes or until the purée doesn't taste of cornflour. Pass through a sieve and cool.

MERINGUE

1. Whisk the egg whites till stiff, gradually adding the sugar during the whisking process.
2. Mix ⅓ of the meringue into the raspberry base, and then fold in another ⅓ followed by the last ⅓ of meringue.

TO ASSEMBLE

1. Preheat oven to 150°C/300°F.
2. Generously line the ramekins twice with butter then coat with a dusting of sugar.
3. Fill the ramekins with the mix, flatten the top with a pallet knife and run your thumb around the edge to remove any excess.
4. Bake for 14 minutes or until risen.
5. Dust the top of the soufflé with icing sugar and serve immediately.

Serves 8

35 minutes

Recipe contributed from the UK

INGREDIENTS

BASE

900g raspberry purée (we like Boiron)

420g caster sugar

90g cornflour

MERINGUE

5 egg whites

50g caster sugar

icing sugar for dusting

NOTES

This is was personal favourite of Queen Elizabeth, according to Queen of our Times, a biography by Robert Hardman, a royal correspondent, journalist and documentarian.

NO BAKE RASPBERRY SWIRL CHEESECAKE

DESSERT

Serves 10-12

35 minutes + chilling

Recipe contributed from the UK

INGREDIENTS

RASPBERRY SAUCE

3 cups fresh or frozen raspberries

50g/¼ cup granulated sugar

1 teaspoon finely grated lemon zest

CRUST

250g packet digestive biscuits

85g/6 tablespoons unsalted butter, melted

1 tablespoon granulated sugar

Pinch of kosher salt

FILLING

450g/16oz cream cheese, softened

150g/¾ cup granulated sugar

1 teaspoon finely grated lemon zest

1 tablespoon lemon juice

1 teaspoon vanilla extract

Pinch of kosher salt

120ml/½ cup sour cream

240ml/1 cup heavy cream, cold

DIRECTIONS

RASPBERRY SAUCE

1. Combine the raspberries, sugar and lemon zest in a medium saucepan over medium heat.
2. Cook, stirring frequently until the mixture comes to a simmer.
3. Turn the heat to medium-high and continue to cook, while stirring, until it is thickened, 4 to 5 minutes.
4. Pour the mixture into a fine mesh sieve set over a bowl, and press the raspberry purée through with a spatula, scraping the underside of the sieve, and chill.

CRUST

1. Add the biscuits to a resealable bag, and crush til you have fine crumbs. Pour the crumbs into a bowl add the butter, sugar and salt, and stir til the butter is evenly distributed.
2. Spray a 9-inch springform pan with cooking spray, and pour the crumb mixture into the pan. Use a measuring cup or flat-bottomed glass to very firmly press the mixture into the bottom and about 1½ inches up the sides of the pan.
3. Refrigerate while you make the filling.

FILLING

1. Combine the cream cheese, sugar, lemon zest and juice, vanilla extract and salt. Mix til smooth and fluffy.
2. Add the sour cream and stir until just combined.
3. With the mixer on low speed, slowly pour in the cream. Turn up to high and whip until thick and fluffy.
4. Pour into the prepared crust and smooth the top. Dot the top with ¼ cup chilled raspberry purée. Using a wooden skewer swirl the purée into the cream cheese mixture.
5. Chill at least 8 hours and up to overnight.

PEACH AND PEAR DUMP CAKE

DESSERT

Serves 8

60 minutes

Recipe contributed from the UK

DIRECTIONS

1. Preheat the oven to 180°C/355°C (fan 160°C 320°F). You'll need a baking dish 18cm x 28cm x 5cm
2. Tip the pear and peaches into a baking dish and toss.
3. In a bowl, mix the flour, baking powder, caster sugar, cornflour and salt thoroughly.
4. Sprinkle this evenly over the tinned fruit, use a fork to spread it out.
5. Lay the sliced butter all over the top, so it will melt all over the cake in the oven – it helps to make sure the butter is close to the edges, so it melts over the sides.
6. Bake for 45-50 mins, until golden brown on top.
7. Serve, with a scoop of ice cream.

NOTES

Super easy, part pudding, part cobbler, part cake. Easy to throw together one-handed and is delicious! Typically made with premade cake mix, but this is better.

INGREDIENTS

415g can of peaches in juice

415g can of pears in juice

210g plain flour

75g caster sugar

1 teaspoon baking powder

1 tablespoon cornflour

1 pinch of salt

100g unsalted butter, cold and thinly sliced

Ice cream, for serving

RHUBARB CUSTARD CAKE

DESSERT

DIRECTIONS

1. Heat oven to fan 180C°C/355°F.
2. Rinse 400g rhubarb and shake off excess water. Trim the ends, then cut into little-finger-size pieces.
3. Place in a shallow dish or a baking tray, tip over 50g caster sugar, toss together, then arrange in a single layer.
4. Cover with foil, then roast for 15 mins. Remove foil. Give everything a little shake, roast for 5 mins more or until tender and the juices are syrupy.
5. Drain off the juices (reserve 3 tablespoons), pressing slightly to remove as much liquid as possible, and let cool.
6. Butter and line a 23cm loose-bottomed or springform cake tin.
7. Cream sugar and butter together, till light and fluffy.
8. Set aside 3 tablespoons of the custard in a bowl.
9. Mix the rest of the custard in with the butter/ sugar mixture and the vanilla.
10. Add each egg individually, beating well between each.
11. Fold in the flour and baking powder until creamy and smooth.
12. Spoon one-third of the mix into the tin, add some of the rhubarb, then dot with one-third more cake mix and spread it out as well as you can. Top with some more rhubarb, then spoon over the remaining cake mix.
13. Scatter the rest of the rhubarb over the batter, then dot the remaining custard over.
14. Bake for 40 mins until risen and golden, then cover with foil and bake for 15-20 mins more.
15. It's ready when a skewer comes out clean.
16. Cool in the tin, pouring the reserved rhubarb juices over the cake.
17. Dust with icing sugar when fully cool.

Serves 16

80 minutes

Recipe contributed from the UK

INGREDIENTS

400g rhubarb

50g caster sugar

250g butter, softened

150g ready-made custard

250g self-raising flour

½ teaspoon baking powder

4 large eggs

1 teaspoon vanilla extract

200g golden caster sugar

icing sugar, for dusting

BLACKBERRY SWIRL CAKE

DESSERT

DIRECTIONS

1. Preheat the oven to 175°C/350°C
2. Lightly butter a 5x9-inch loaf pan and line with parchment, leaving a 2-inch overhang on all sides; butter parchment.
3. In a food processor puree blackberries + 2 tablespoons sugar.
4. In a medium bowl, whisk together flour, salt, and baking powder.
5. In a large bowl, using an electric mixer, beat together butter and 1 ¼ cups sugar until light and fluffy, 5 minutes.
6. Add eggs and vanilla and beat to combine.
7. With mixer on low, add flour mixture in 3 additions, alternating with sour cream, beginning and ending with flour mixture.
8. Transfer half the batter to pan and dot with 1/2 cup blackberry puree. Repeat with remaining batter and puree. With a skewer, swirl batter and puree together.
9. Bake for 75 minutes, or till a toothpick inserted in centre of cake comes out clean. Let cool completely before slicing.

Serves 8

60 minutes

Recipe contributed from the UK

INGREDIENTS

½ cup unsalted butter, softened

1 1/3 cups/6oz blackberries

1 ¼ cup plus **2 tablespoons** sugar

1 ½ cup all-purpose flour

½ teaspoon coarse salt

¼ teaspoon baking powder

2 large eggs, lightly beaten

½ teaspoon pure vanilla extract

½ cup sour cream, room temperature

PEAR CAKE

DESSERT

DIRECTIONS

1. Heat oven to fan 175C°C/350°F.
2. Prep your pan: Line the bottom of the pan with parchment paper and grease or spray a round springform baking pan. A 10 x 3 inch deep pan works well.
3. Peel, core and thinly slice your pears.
4. In an electric mixer bowl, cream together the sugar and butter for a minute or two, until well combined.
5. Mix in the vanilla, lemon zest and eggs.
6. Add in the baking powder, sifted flour and a pinch of salt. Mix until just combined.
7. Alternate between adding a bit of the ½ cup of milk and ⅓ cup oil while mixing on low speed till very well combined.
8. Pour the batter into the prepped pan.
9. Layer the sliced pears over the batter and sprinkle the brown sugar on top.
10. Bake in a pre-heated oven for 40 minutes, then cover with foil and bake for another 10-15 minutes until a wooden skewer comes out clean.
11. Remove the cake from the oven and allow to cool.
12. Dust with icing sugar and lemon and serve!

Serves 16

80 minutes

Recipe contributed from the UK

INGREDIENTS

2¼ cups all-purpose flour sifted

1½ cup caster sugar

½ cup unsalted butter soft

⅓ cup canola oil or vegetable oil

2 teaspoons baking powder

2 teaspoons vanilla extract

4 whole eggs

½ cup milk

3 ripe pears peeled, cored and sliced

⅛ teaspoon salt (just a pinch)

1 teaspoon lemon zest

1 teaspoon icing sugar for dusting

¼ cup brown sugar

BASIC POUND CAKE

DESSERT

DIRECTIONS

1. Preheat the oven to 175°C/350°F
2. Butter and flour a 6-cup (8.5x4.5-inch) loaf pan; set aside.
3. Using an electric mixer on high speed, beat butter and sugar until light and fluffy.
4. Add eggs one at a time, beating well after each addition.
5. Add vanilla and salt.
6. With mixer on low, gradually add flour, beating just until combined (do not overmix).
7. Bake until a toothpick inserted in centre of cake comes out clean, about 1 hour (tent with aluminium foil if browning too quickly).
8. Let cool in pan 15 minutes. Invert onto a wire rack, and turn upright to cool completely.
9. Serve lightly toasted with whipped cream or greek yoghurt and berries.

Serves 8

75 minutes

Recipe contributed from the USA

INGREDIENTS

1 cup unsalted butter, softened

2 cups all-purpose flour

1 cup sugar

4 large eggs

2 teaspoons pure vanilla extract

½ teaspoon salt

CHOCOLATE BANOFFEE PIE

DESSERT

DIRECTIONS

1. Put the digestive biscuits in a ziplock bag and gently crush with a rolling pin, ensuring the crumb is even and fine.
2. Mix with the melted butter, and press into the base and sides of a 20cm spring form cake pan, or a pie dish.
3. Gently melt the chocolate in a heat-proof mixing bowl over a pan of simmering water (or a double boiler, if you have one).
4. Mix in the caramel and beat until smooth.
5. Spread over the base, and chill for an hour or so.
6. Slice the bananas, set a handful aside. Lay the rest across the chocolate mix.
7. Whip the cream, and spoon over the bananas.
8. Decorate with the remaining bananas and dust liberally with cocoa powder. Chill until ready to serve.

Serves 12

65 minutes

Recipe contributed from the UK

INGREDIENTS

85g butter, melted

250g digestive biscuits

150g good quality milk chocolate

200ml double/heavy cream

1 tin of Carnation Caramel

2 bananas

4 large eggs

cocoa powder, for dusting

CHOCOLATE GUINNESS CAKE

DESSERT

DIRECTIONS

1. Preheat the oven to 180°C/355°F.
2. Butter and line a 23cm springform tin.
3. Pour the Guinness into a large wide saucepan, add the butter and heat until the butter's melted.
4. Whisk in the cocoa and sugar.
5. In a separate bowl, beat the sour cream, eggs and vanilla.
6. Pour into the buttery beer pan and whisk in the flour and bicarbonate of soda.
7. Pour the batter into the greased and lined tin and bake for 45 minutes to an hour.
8. Leave to cool completely in the tin on a cooling rack.
9. Lightly whip the cream cheese until smooth, sieve over the icing sugar and cornflour and then beat to combine.
10. Add the double cream and beat until you have a spreadable consistency.
11. Slice the cake in half, into even layers.
12. Spread a thin layer of cream cheese icing on the bottom layer, and add the strawberries on the inside. Add the top layer, and ice the top of the cake.

Serves 12

90 minutes

Recipe contributed from the UK

INGREDIENTS

250ml Guinness

250g unsalted butter

75g cocoa powder

400g caster sugar

150ml sour cream

2 large eggs

1 tablespoon vanilla extract

275g plain flour

2½ teaspoons bicarbonate of soda

300g cream cheese

150g icing sugar

2 teaspoons cornflour

125ml double cream

handful strawberries, sliced

NOTES

This cake is so easy, and so delicious! It works well as cupcakes, or as a single-layer cake. Sometimes I like to add a whipped milk chocolate ganache to the middle layer for extra decadence. For the ganache, finely chop 200g of good-quality milk chocolate in a heatproof bowl. Heat 100ml of cream, to just barely a simmer (watch for tiny bubbles around the edge of the pan - do not let boil). Pour the cream over the chocolate and leave the chocolate to melt for 5 minutes or so. Slowly stir to combine, until smooth. Put in fridge to set. Once set, use an electric whisk to whip the ganache until light, fluffy and spreadable. Nom!

OLD-FASHIONED CHOCOLATE CAKE

DESSERT

DIRECTIONS

1. Mix the cocoa powder with some hot water from the kettle to make a runny paste and leave to cool slightly.
2. Cream together the sugar and margarine until light and fluffy.
3. Beat the eggs and add them a bit at a time to the mixture, beating well.
4. Add some of the flour to stop it curdling.
5. Mix the cocoa powder paste into the batter and then fold in the flour and a few drops of vanilla essence.
6. Put into 2 sandwich cake tins - mine are 7cm. Grease them slightly and line the base if you can be bothered!
7. Bake at Gas Mark 4 (180°C/355°F) for 25 - 30 minutes.
8. Prepare the filling by creaming the butter and icing sugar plus cocoa powder and a few drops of milk and sandwich the cake halves together.
9. If you double up the ingredients you can use to top the cake too. I always had to melt chocolate for the top - the family demanded it!
10. Decorate with smarties or whatever your family demands....

Serves 12

55 minutes

Recipe contributed from the UK

INGREDIENTS

150g caster sugar

150g margarine

150g self raising flour

3 medium eggs

4 tablespoons of cocoa powder

Vanilla essence

75g icing sugar

100g salt-free butter, room temp

1 tablespoon cocoa powder

Drop of milk

Dark chocolate and smarties

ABOUT

This makes a lovely moist cake. Don't make the cocoa powder mixture too runny - just enough to resemble thick double cream. I'm Mikaere's grandma on Sam's side. This cake was a Hulance classic for every birthday or special occasion and is still my most popular cake. The recipe came from a very old M&S cookbook and has been adapted over the years - it must be about 40 years old! I have lots of birthday photos showing the candles being blown out on this particular cake from years back. Try it - you won't be disappointed. It's really chocolatey!

LOCKDOWN BANANA LOAF

DESSERT

DIRECTIONS

1. Preheat the oven to 180°C/355°F.
2. Butter a 9x5x3-inch loaf pan.
3. Using an electric mixer on high speed, beat butter and sugar until light and fluffy.
4. Add eggs and beat to incorporate.
5. Add vanilla and salt.
6. In a medium bowl, whisk together flour, baking soda, and salt.
7. Add to the butter mixture and mix until just combined.
8. Add bananas, sour cream, and vanilla; mix to combine.
9. Toss nuts and chocolate chips in a tablespoon of flour to stop them from sinking and mix into the batter.
10. Pour into prepared pan, bake for 70 minutes until a cake tester inserted into the centre of the cake comes out clean.
11. Let rest in pan for 10 minutes, then turn out onto a rack to cool.

Serves 8

90 minutes

Recipe contributed from the UK

INGREDIENTS

½ cup butter, softened

1 cup sugar

2 large eggs

1 ½ cups all-purpose flour

1 teaspoon baking soda

1 teaspoon vanilla extract

½ teaspoon salt

1 cup mashed very ripe bananas

½ cup sour cream or greek yoghurt

½ cup chopped walnuts

½ cup chocolate chips

CHOCOLATE SELF SAUCING PUDDING

DESSERT

DIRECTIONS

1. Preheat the oven to fan 150°C/300°F. Grease the inside of an ovenproof dish (or ramekins) with a little butter and set aside.
2. Cream the measured butter with 225g/8oz of the soft light brown sugar until pale and light, scraping down the sides of the bowl with a rubber spatula from time to time.
3. Gradually add the beaten eggs, mixing well between each addition and then add the vanilla extract and mix again to combine.
4. Sift the flour, 40g/1¾oz cocoa, bicarbonate of soda and a pinch of salt into the mixture and mix again until just combined.
5. Add the milk and mix again until smooth. Spoon the mixture into the prepared dish and level with the back of a spoon.
6. In a small bowl mix together the remaining 75g/2½oz soft light brown sugar, 2 tablespoons of cocoa powder and 6 tablespoons hot water. Spoon this chocolatey syrup over the chocolate sponge mixture and place the dish in a large, deep roasting tin.
7. Boil the kettle and pour boiling water into the tin, around the dish so that the water comes halfway up the sides of the dish. Carefully slide the roasting tin into the oven on the middle shelf.
8. Bake for about 45 minutes, or until the pudding is well-risen, the top is nicely cracked and a skewer inserted into the middle of the pudding comes out with a moist crumb.
9. Dust with icing sugar and serve immediately with double cream.

Serves 6

60 minutes

Recipe contributed from the UK

INGREDIENTS

175g/6oz unsalted butter, at room temperature, plus extra for greasing

300g/10½oz soft light brown sugar

3 large eggs, beaten

1 teaspoon vanilla extract

175g/6oz plain flour

40g/1¾oz cocoa powder, plus

2 tablespoons cocoa powder

1 teaspoon bicarbonate of soda

pinch salt

3 tablespoons milk

icing sugar, for dusting

double cream, to serve

CHERRY CLAFOUTIS

DESSERT

DIRECTIONS

1. Preheat the oven to 180°C/350°F.
2. In a large bowl, mix together flour, sugar and salt. Whisk in the eggs, the cold milk (slowly) then the warm butter (add ¾ teaspoon of almond extract for a little "je ne sais quoi").
3. Grease a round baking dish or iron skillet and arrange the pitted cherries in the dish. Pour over the batter until the cherries are just covered.
4. Bake until puffed and golden (around 40 minutes). Turn the oven off, leave the cake inside for 10 more minutes.
5. Dust the clafoutis with icing sugar and serve lukewarm.

NOTES

You can replace the cherries with any other fruit in season, Raspberries are great! Recipe submitted by Delphine Pages (<3)

Serves 4-6

60 minutes

Recipe contributed from Austin, TX, USA

INGREDIENTS

500g/1lb cherries

2 tablespoons flour

5 tablespoons sugar

3 eggs

400ml/13.5oz milk

30g/2 tablespoons butter

1 pinch of salt

¾ teaspoon almond extract, optional

PUDDING GOODIE

DESSERT

Serves 20

30 minutes

Recipe contributed from the USA

DIRECTIONS

1. Rest the cream cheese at room temp to soften.
2. With a fork, mix together bisquick and brown sugar.
3. Add firm margarine to the mixture - diced – then mix with a fork until the margarine is in the size of peas. This will not be a smooth consistency but rather flaky.
4. Press crust into a 13 X 9 X 2 inch pan. Sprinkle chocolate chips over crust and press down on the chips to embed in the crust.
5. Bake in a 175°C/350°F oven til light brown, about 10 minutes. The butter will look melted but the chips won't. Allow to cool.
6. Mix ½ of the cool whip, cream cheese and powdered sugar with an electric beater til well mixed.
7. Drop small dollops of cream cheese mix onto the crust, and then spread flat evenly over the crust (this helps the crust to stay on the bottom of the pan and not be mix with the layer).
8. Place 2 ½ cups of milk into a large bowl and add chocolate pudding mix. Beat til it thickens.
9. Pour the chocolate pudding mix over the cream cheese layer.
10. Place 2 ½ cups of milk into a large bowl and add vanilla pudding mix. Beat until it thickens.
11. Pour this over the chocolate pudding spreading it evenly over the layer.
12. When the vanilla layer has set, gently add dollops of the remaining cool whip over the vanilla pudding, and spread with the back of a spoon evenly over the top.
13. Chill for several hours before serving.
14. OPTIONAL: Add chopped nuts, crushed cookies, chocolate chips or anything else you'd like for a topping over the cool whip.

INGREDIENTS

¼ cup Bisquick

¼ cup packed brown sugar

3 tablespoons firm butter

170g/6oz chocolate chips

1 cup powdered sugar

5 cups milk

225g/8oz cream cheese – softened

1 large (2 small) INSTANT vanilla pudding packet

1 large (2 small) INSTANT chocolate pudding packet

1 large (biggest they make) Cool Whip

ABOUT

Contributed by Kristi Ebert, whose grandson, Rhett, was born with NKH Nov. 3rd 2018. She says "This recipe was a favorite of the athletics teams at the High School where I taught for 38 years. That tradition has continued as student athletes became coaches and offered treats for their teams."

ICECREAM PIE

DESSERT

DIRECTIONS

1. If you're making your own pie crusts, add the Oreos to a food processor or blender and grind into fine crumbs. You do not need to remove the filling from the Oreos. Add the Oreo crumbs to a bowl and combine with the melted butter. Press the mixture into your pie pan and press into an even layer on the bottom and up the sides. Chill for 30 minutes.
2. Smash the Oreo cookies into crumbs and mix with ice cream and Cool Whip/cream.
3. Scoop into Oreo pie crusts.
4. Freeze until firm.
5. Just before serving, top with more Cool Whip and Oreo pieces.

ABOUT

Recipe submitted by Tanya Graves, "My husband has been making this for our youngest daughter for her birthday. It since has been a tradition for her."

Serves 6-8

15 minutes + freeze time

Recipe contributed from the USA

INGREDIENTS

1 packet of Oreo cookies

1 (8 oz) Cool Whip (or double cream whipped, if you're not in the US)

2L/½ gal vanilla ice-cream softened

3 premade Oreo pie crusts (or, if you'd prefer homemade, 24 Oreos and 4 tablespoons of butter)

AMBROSIA

DESSERT

DIRECTIONS

1. Chop your marshmallows in half, drain the pears and peaches and chop the fruit into bite-sized pieces.
2. In a different bowl, whip the cream until it forms soft peaks (be careful not to overbeat).
3. Gently fold the strawberry yoghurt into the whipped cream, till well incorporated.
4. Add the marshmallows and fruit, and fold in to combine.
5. Spoon this mix into a large serving bowl, or individual ramekins.
6. Sprinkle with crumbled flake pieces and chill before serving.

ABOUT

This is a very kiwi dessert, often shared around Christmas time, perfect for potlucks. It's also very adaptable, use whatever fruit you have on hand!

Serves 10

30 minutes

Recipe contributed from Aotearoa/New Zealand

INGREDIENTS

400ml/13.5 floz double/heavy cream

375ml/13.5 floz strawberry yoghurt

220g/7oz soft marshmallows (halved)

2 chocolate flake bars

1 banana

1 punnet of strawberries

1 can peaches

1 can pears

CHOCOLATE CUPS
DESSERT

DIRECTIONS

1. Very finely chop 200g of high-quality milk chocolate. Chop as finely as possible. Place in a glass/pyrex bowl (not plastic).
2. In a saucepan, heat 100g (definitely grams, and not mls, the weight ratio is important here) of cream. Do NOT let it boil, you want to heat the cream until you start to see tiny bubbles or ripples around the edge.
3. Pour the hot cream over the chocolate pieces.
4. Cover the bowl and let it sit for two minutes.
5. Slowly stir the mix with a spatula (NOT a whisk, we don't want to introduce too much air) to combine, until completely silky smooth. Do not stir too quickly or vigorously. Take your time.
6. Pour into ramekins (or glasses) and chill in the fridge.
7. Just before serving, slice your strawberries and set aside.
8. Whip the remaining cream until soft peaks form (be careful not to over beat).
9. Using a vegetable peeler, peel the chocolate to create chocolate ribbons.
10. In your ramekins, add the strawberries on top of the chocolate base, add a dollop of whipped cream and sprinkle chocolate ribbons on the top.

NOTES

So easy and delicious, and it's easy to prep ahead of time (making it perfect for dinner parties) and it looks really elegant and impressive, and isn't too heavy. If you'd prefer to use dark chocolate, the ratio is 1:1 with cream (ie, 200g dark chocolate with 200g double cream). If you would like to try white chocolate, the ratio is 3:1 (300g white chocolate with 100g double cream). If you're feeling adventurous, you can also top with crushed candied nuts - it's a bit more work but oh la it is tasty!

Serves 4

15 minutes + freeze time

Recipe contributed from the UK

INGREDIENTS

200g high-quality milk chocolate

50g high-quality milk chocolate (for topping)

100g double/heavy whipping cream (for chocolate base)

100ml double/heavy cream (for topping)

Handful of strawberries

DRINKS

BEE'S KNEES
COCKTAIL

COCKTAIL

1. Add the gin, lemon juice and honey syrup into a shaker with ice and shake until well-chilled.
2. Strain into a chilled cocktail glass.
3. Garnish with a lemon twist.

HONEY SYRUP

1. Taste the honey you're using and adjust the proportion of honey to water accordingly; milder honey (like clover) may be best with a two to one ratio of honey to water.
2. Add honey + water into a small saucepan over medium heat.
3. Stir until the honey is dissolved.
4. Allow to cool and transfer to an airtight container. Syrup will keep, refrigerated, for up to 1 month.

Serves 2

Recipe contributed from the UK

INGREDIENTS

COCKTAIL

120ml/4oz gin

40ml/ 1½oz fresh lemon juice

30 ml/ 1oz an ounce of honey syrup

Garnish: lemon twist

HONEY SYRUP

1/2 cup honey (adjust to taste)

1/2 cup water

ABOUT

According to the laws of aerodynamics, Bumblebee's shouldn't have the ability to fly. But they don't know that, and they do. Similarly, NKH parents are told their babies won't live, but they do.

Which is why the NKH community has taken on the symbol of the bumblebee. We raise this drink to all our little bumblebees, to their health. May they always fly high.

ELLY-QUENT

COCKTAIL

DIRECTIONS

1. In a gin glass, add several ice cubes.
2. Squeeze the lime over the ice.
3. Pour over the apple sourz, gin, apple juice and cranberry.
4. Top with gingerbeer, and garnish with mint.

ABOUT

Before she moved to London, Elly frequented a bar in Newmarket, in New Zealand with a few very good friends. The bartender there named a drink after her (a play on eloquent), and they drank this all the time. It was a ridiculous time, and this is a very sweet and nostalgic pink cocktail!

Serves 4

Recipe contributed from the UK

INGREDIENTS

75ml apple sourz

75ml gin

75ml apple juice

75ml cranberry juice

½ a lime, quartered

Ginger beer to top

Mint garnish

GRAPEFRUIT ROSÉ SPRITZ

COCKTAIL

Serves 1

Recipe contributed from the UK

DIRECTIONS

1. Combine the rosé vodka, grapefruit juice, sparkling rosé, elderflower liqueur and lemon juice in a stirring glass.
2. Add ice to fill halfway.
3. Stir for 10 seconds, and strain into a coupe glass.
4. Top with thyme sprig and a slice of grapefruit and serve.

INGREDIENTS

30ml/1oz rosé vodka

30ml/1oz freshly squeezed, strained pink grapefruit juice

30ml/1oz dry sparkling rosé

15ml/½ oz elderflower liqueur

Few drops of lemon juice, to taste

Sliced grapefruit and thyme sprig for garnish

CUCUMBER AND ELDERFLOWER SPRITZER

COCKTAIL

DIRECTIONS

1. Roughly chop the cucumber into a few chunks, then add to a blender or food processor with the wine and elderflower cordial.
2. Whizz until well blended, then pour through a sieve set over a large bowl or jug.
3. Tip the contents of the sieve back into the machine, whizz again until pulpy, then sieve again into the liquid already collected.
4. Add 1-2 tbsp of the cucumber pulp from the sieve into the liquid and discard the rest. Chill for at least 20 minutes.
5. To serve, fill glasses with a few ice cubes, lime and cucumber slices. Half fill with the cucumber base, then top with soda water. Garnish with basil.

Serves 4

Recipe contributed from Australia

INGREDIENTS

1 cucumber, ends trimmed

½ bottle white wine

200ml/7oz elderflower cordial

2 1L bottles soda water, chilled

Basil leaves, for garnish

Lime slices, for garnish

TURKISH DELIGHT VODKA

COCKTAIL/GIFT

DIRECTIONS

1. Decant 100ml from the vodka bottle (save for other drinks, perfect for a cocktail).
2. Mix the rose water and caster sugar til the sugar dissolves, then pour into the vodka bottle using a funnel.
3. Wash any sugar off the Turkish delight, and add to the bottle.
4. Screw on the lid and leave to stand for up to a month, swirling occasionally until the Turkish delight dissolves.
5. Serve with soda water and ice, or decant into smaller bottles, adding extra Turkish delight to give as gifts!

Serves many

Recipe contributed from the UK

INGREDIENTS

1L bottle vodka

1 teaspoon rosewater

1 teaspoon caster sugar

100g/3.5oz Turkish delight, chopped, plus a little extra for packaging

BASIL & LILLET SPRITZ

COCKTAIL

DIRECTIONS

1. In a shaker, combine lillet and 4-5 basil leaves together and shake vigorously with ice for 30 seconds, with the aim of infusing the lillet with the basil.
2. Strain into a glass, remove the broken ice chips and basil leaves.
3. Add ice and top with the bubbles and a squeeze of lime.
4. Garnish with remaining basil.

Serves 1

Recipe contributed from France

INGREDIENTS

30ml/1oz lillet blanc, a French aperitif

5-8 basil leaves

30ml/1oz of a nice champagne, or prosecco

squeeze of lime

FROSÉ
COCKTAIL

DIRECTIONS

1. Pour the bottle of rosé into a deep roasting tin and put it in the freezer overnight.
2. The next day, hull and halve the strawberries. then mix with the sugar and leave to sit for 30 mins until the strawberries release their juices.
3. Blend the frozen rosé, strawberries, sugar and lemon juice together, then divide between glasses.
4. Serve with a strawberry garnish.

Serves 4-6

Recipe contributed from the UK

INGREDIENTS

1 bottle dry rosé

300g strawberries

50g caster sugar

juice of 1 lemon

FROZEN MANGO DAIQUIRI

COCKTAIL

DIRECTIONS

1. Put the rum, mango liqueur/gin, lemon juice, mango and a very generous handful of ice in a high-powered blender (one that's capable of crushing ice).
2. Blend until smooth.
3. Pour into a margarita glass.
4. Garnish with a slice of mango and basil.

Serves 1

Recipe contributed from the UK

INGREDIENTS

50ml white rum

25ml mango liqueur or mango gin

10ml lemon juice

½ ripe mango, peeled, stoned and diced

Basil sprig, garnish

FROZEN PEACH BELLINI

COCKTAIL

DIRECTIONS

1. If using fresh peaches, dice and place in the freezer until well frozen.
2. Add the frozen peaches, sugar, and a handful of crushed ice in a blender. Blend until smooth.
3. Add the prosecco and pulse until well incorporated.
4. Divide into glasses and top with a peach slice.

Serves 4

Recipe contributed from the USA

INGREDIENTS

3 cups frozen diced peaches

1½ tablespoons caster sugar

3 cups prosecco

1 cup crushed ice

SAM'S WORLD FAMOUS OLD FASHIONED

COCKTAIL

Serves 1

Recipe contributed from the UK

DIRECTIONS

1. Add the sugar and the bitters to a whiskey tumbler, add a splash of water and mix until the sugar dissolves.
2. Fill the glass with ice and add your bourbon.
3. Stir the mixture to dissolve as much sugar as you can into the bourbon.
4. Garnish with a twist of orange peel

INGREDIENTS

2 teaspoons granulated sugar

3 or 4 dashes of angostura bitters

A decent bourbon

Ice

Orange peel

ABOUT

If you're a whiskey drinker and been a dinner guest at the Hulance House, it's likely you've enjoyed one of these. Sam's well known for his deliciously potent old fashioneds!

NOTES

To make smoother old fashioned prepare some simple syrup in advance and use that instead of mixing on the fly. At home my old fashioneds sport about 140ml of whiskey, it can be strong AF but it's ok to water it down if you need. For after-dinner guests, my old fashioneds are usually the last nail in the coffin before they stagger home. For the hardcore, if you've got a good absinthe - add a tablespoon of absinthe to the tumbler and line it before step one. It'll add another layer of sweetness, and kick to the drink. This is less old fashioned and more sazerac!

JACOBITE NEGRONI

COCKTAIL

Serves 1

Recipe contributed via the Isle of Skye, Scotland

INGREDIENTS

25ml 57° Skye, Earth & Sea Gin

25ml Campari

25ml Cocchi sweet vermouth

Orange wheel, for garnish

DIRECTIONS

1. Add all ingredients to a glass, fill with ice and stir.
2. Add an orange wheel to garnish.

ABOUT

Shared very kindly by Breege, whose son Rauirí went to Small Steps with Mikaere. 57° Skye was co-founded by Breege's husband, Shane.

HANKY PANKY

COCKTAIL

Serves 1

Recipe contributed via the Isle of Skye, Scotland

INGREDIENTS

50ml 57° Skye, Earth & Sea Gin

40ml Cocchi sweet vermouth

5ml Fernet Branca

DIRECTIONS

1. Add all ingredients to mixing glass with ice and stir well.
2. Strain into chilled coupe or martini glass.
3. Garnish with twist of orange and a cherry.

RHUBARB FIZZ

COCKTAIL

DIRECTIONS

1. Pour gin into an ice-filled glass, and stir in 50ml of rhubarb cordial.
2. Top with sparkling wine.
3. Serve!

NOTES

This one is good for rhubarb season. There is something delightful about drinking this from rhubarb you've grown yourself!

Serves 1

Recipe contributed from the UK

INGREDIENTS

25ml gin

75ml sparkling wine

50ml rhubarb cordial (below)

ice

RHUBARB CORDIAL

NON-ALCOHOLIC

DIRECTIONS

1. To a large saucepan add 300ml water. Bring to a simmer then add the zest and juice of both the orange and the lemon along with the rhubarb and the ginger. Cook the mixture over a medium heat until the rhubarb is falling apart.
2. Pour the mixture through a sieve lined with muslin into a clean heatproof jug then transfer to sterilised bottles.
3. Keeps in the fridge for up to 1 month.
4. Serve approx. 25ml of cordial per 100ml sparkling water, or in Rhubarb fizz.

Makes approx. 500ml

Recipe contributed from the UK

INGREDIENTS

300g golden caster sugar

450g rhubarb, chopped

1 slice fresh root ginger, peeled

zest and juice 1 orange

zest and juice 1 lemon

PEACH ICED TEA

NON-ALCOHOLIC

DIRECTIONS

1. Tip the sugar into a pan with 250ml water. Bring to the boil slowly, ensuring the sugar is fully dissolved.
2. Add the chopped peaches and cook until very soft.
3. Remove from the heat, mash the peaches with a fork, and leave to infuse for 60 minutes.
4. Sieve the syrup through a fine sieve into a jug, mashing the fruit to release all the liquid. The peach syrup will keep in the fridge for one week.
5. Put the teabags in a large heatproof jug and pour over 2 litres of boiling water. Leave to steep for 4 mins, then carefully remove the teabags. Leave to cool, then transfer to the fridge until chilled.
6. Add ice to a collins glass, fill a third of the glass with the peach syrup, a third with the chilled tea, and top with sparkling water. Add peach slices to serve.

Serves 12

Recipe contributed from the USA

INGREDIENTS

200g/7oz granulated sugar

5 ripe peaches, 4 stoned and chopped, 1 sliced to serve

4 teabags

MULLED APPLE JUICE

NON-ALCOHOLIC

DIRECTIONS

1. In a saucepan, simmer the apple juice with the strips of orange peel, star anise, cinnamon stick and cloves for about 5-10 minutes until all the flavours have infused.
2. Sweeten with sugar or honey to taste.
3. Ladle the mulled apple juice into mugs.
4. Garnish each with apple slices, cloves, cinnamon sticks and fresh rosemary.

ABOUT

Perfect for those who are, for whatever reason, unable to enjoy the seasonal mulled wine that pops up in the festive season. This recipe is so easy to make, and well delicious. If you are not a fan of aniseed, leave the star anise out.

Serves 8

Recipe contributed from the UK

INGREDIENTS

1L apple juice

1 cinnamon stick

1 star anise

3 cloves

strips of orange peel

sugar or honey, to taste

Apple slices, for garnish

Cinnamon sticks, for garnish

Star anise, for garnish

Fresh rosemary, for garnish

GINGER LEMON FIZZ

NON-ALCOHOLIC

DIRECTIONS

1. Place the ginger, sugar and lemon slices in a pan with 150-200ml water.
2. Bring to the boil, then cook until the sugar dissolves.
3. Take off the heat, leave to cool, then press through a sieve.
4. To serve, pour into a pitcher and top up with sparkling water and extra lemon slices.

Serves 4

Recipe contributed from New Zealand

INGREDIENTS

50g fresh root ginger

300g caster sugar

2 lemons, sliced, plus extra to serve

Sparkling water

WATERMELON LEMONADE

NON-ALCOHOLIC

DIRECTIONS

1. Cut the top off the watermelon and hollow it out using a large spoon, fishing out any pips along the way.
2. Mash the flesh through a sieve into a bowl. Put the flesh in a blender with the lemon juice and sugar, whizz to a purée, then stir in the soda.
3. Heap some ice into the hollowed-out watermelon and fill it with the lemonade mixture.
4. Serve the rest in a jug with ice, lime slices and mint.

Serves 8

Recipe contributed from the UK

INGREDIENTS

1 large or 2 small watermelons

200ml lemon juice

100g golden caster sugar

1L bottle soda water

1 lime, cut into slices

small handful mint

crushed ice

PINK LEMONADE

NON-ALCOHOLIC

DIRECTIONS

1. Place the sugar, raspberries, sliced lemons and sliced orange into a large saucepan and pour over 350ml cold water.
2. Bring to the boil, stirring often, then leave to cool.
3. Pour through a sieve, pressing down with a spoon to extract all the juices.
4. To serve, pour a little into a glass and top up with sparkling or still water, ice and mint.

Serves 8

Recipe contributed from the UK

INGREDIENTS

300g caster sugar

500g raspberries

1 ½ sliced lemons

1 orange, sliced

fresh mint to garnish

EASY GINGERBEER

NON-ALCOHOLIC

DIRECTIONS

1. Place the ginger and lemon in a bowl, pour over 300ml water and blitz with a hand blender until very smooth.
2. Strain through a sieve into a bowl, compress the pulp to remove as much liquid as you can.
3. Add the sugar to the bowl and blitz again.
4. Decant into a bottle. Chill until ready to use.
5. To serve, add two or three fingers to a glass, add ice and lemonade or sparkling water before serving.

Serves 6

Recipe contributed from Australia

INGREDIENTS

100g ginger, scrubbed and roughly chopped

1 lemon, chopped

100g light muscovado sugar

1L bottle chilled lemonade or sparkling water, to serve

CUCUMBER GIMLET

NON-ALCOHOLIC MOCKTAIL

DIRECTIONS

1. If you don't have simple syrup on hand, add ½ cup granulated sugar and ½ cup water to a small saucepan over medium heat. Stir until sugar is dissolved. Allow to cool to room temperature, then pour into a glass jar and seal tightly with a lid. Simple syrup will keep, refrigerated, for about one month.
2. Add cucumber to a shaker, and muddle (meaning, with a muddler (similar to a pestle), press down lightly and give a few gentle twists).
3. Add the club soda, lime juice, simple syrup and ice, and shake well.
4. Serve in a rocks glass with cucumber ribbons and sprig of rosemary.

Serves 1

Recipe contributed from the UK

INGREDIENTS

40ml/1.5oz club soda

4-5 slices of muddled cucumber

30ml/1oz fresh lime juice

30ml/1oz simple syrup

ice

rosemary sprig

SAM'S ICED TEA

NON-ALCOHOLIC

DIRECTIONS

1. Slice the lemon.
2. Add the teabags, sugar and half the lemon slices into a large heatproof jug or pitcher.
3. Add 1L of freshly boiled water and let it brew for 5 minutes.
4. Pop the other slices of lemon back in the fridge, these are for serving.
5. Stir well, then discard the teabags and lemon slices. Let it cool to room temperature before moving it to the fridge.
6. When you're in need of a refreshing glass of something, grab some ice, some slices of lemon and pour away.

Serves 4

Recipe contributed from the UK

INGREDIENTS

4 teabags

1 lemon, sliced

1 ½ tablespoons sugar if you fancy

NOTES

I use typical black tea (like Yorkshire, an English Breakfast blend), but you could try using different blends such as an Earl Grey or Darjeeling, white teas or even fruit teas. You can also play with garnishes. Frozen berries are great to throw in fruity teas (or even frozen mango, or pineapple).

There are many garnish options: slices of stone fruit work really well, as does grated ginger and herbs (sprigs of rosemary, mint, basil, thyme etc). Watermelon, cucumber, as well as other citrus fruit (limes, oranges, grapefruit) work a treat for variation and colour. It's a very flexible recipe. We've tried cucumber, blueberry and fresh mint with chamomile, or white tea with fresh peaches and rosemary. Still like the classic version best, though!

HOMEMADE LEMONADE

NON-ALCOHOLIC

Serves 12-15

Recipe contributed from the UK

INGREDIENTS

200g/7oz of sugar

9 lemons

2.5L Water

Garnishes for serving

DIRECTIONS

1. Make the simple syrup in a large pan. Add 200g sugar to 400ml of water and slowly bring to a boil while stirring every so often. Make sure the sugar is all dissolved and there is no grittiness. Once dissolved take off the heat to cool.
2. While you're making the simple syrup juice all the lemons. While the syrup is cooling add the lemon juice. I like to add some of the pulp in too.
3. Give it a stir and add in more water. I usually add in 500ml at a time, typically up to around 2 litres tasting as I go to make sure it's not too sweet or tart. If you like it strong don't add in as much water. If it's too tart, you can add more water or make more syrup to add.
4. Once you've got a balance you're happy with, and the lemonade has cooled, decant it into a pitcher or bottle and pop in the fridge to chill so it's ready to sip at your desire.
5. Serve with ice and lemon slices, or add to a lemonade pitcher with fruit garnishes (lemons, oranges, limes, berries, mint, edible flowers etc).

MOCKTAIL STATION

NON-ALCOHOLIC MOCKTAILS

INGREDIENTS

- A selection of glass types (collins, flutes and margarita or gin glasses are quite fun).
- An ice bucket with ice cubes and/or crushed ice.
- A selection of juices (apple, cranberry and mango are good choices). If you want to be fancy, decant them into matching glass bottles.
- A selection of mixers (lemonade, ginger beer, soda water, appletiser etc).
- A selection of cordials/syrups (elderflower cordial, simple syrup, rhubarb, lychee, ginger etc).
- A selection of garnishes: lemon/lime slices, berries (strawberries, blackberries, blueberries), herbs (basil, rosemary, mint, thyme, lemon grass etc), fruits (cherries, lychees, passionfruit pulp, watermelon cubes, pomegranate etc), cucumber ribbons, edible flowers, dehydrated fruits.

Serves many

Recipe contributed from the UK

DIRECTIONS

This is great for parties, like baby showers, and is such a fun thing to do. The key is a coordinated aesthetic (decant everything into matching glassware and pitchers). Set up your station on a table out of the way, with good access. Garnishes up front, bottles at back. Make sure you provide spoons/mini tongs for the garnishes and ice. Label everything for ease of use!

WATERMELON SLUSHY

NON-ALCOHOLIC

DIRECTIONS

1. Hours before slushy drinking, cut the watermelon into chunks and remove the skin and seeds. Place half the watermelon wedges into a large freezable bag and freezer for a 3-4 hours.
2. Once frozen, blend the frozen watermelon with the rest of the watermelon, strawberries and lime juice until smooth and slushy.
3. Pour into glasses and sip through a straw.

Serves 6

Recipe contributed from the UK

INGREDIENTS

1 small watermelon

225g ripe strawberries, hulled

juice of 2 limes

CHOCBANANA MILKSHAKE

SUPER GOOD

DIRECTIONS

1. Peel and cut bananas, add in a single layer to a freezer safe container and freeze for at least 20 minutes.
2. Add the bananas, ice cream, cocoa and whole milk to a blender.
3. Blend for 12 to 18 seconds until all is mixed.
4. Serve immediately with whipped cream and a sprinkle of cocoa powder.

Serves 2

Recipe contributed from the UK

INGREDIENTS

2 bananas

1 ½ cups vanilla ice cream

½ cup whole milk

1 teaspoon cocoa powder

NOTES

This recipe is very flexible, add strawberries for a berry shake, or switch out the cocoa for half a teaspoon of cinnamon. If you're not into ice cream, leave it out and triple the bananas (or use frozen banana slices, if you have the spare time). Dairy-free versions work just as well!

BLENDS

THE BLENDED DIET
JUST A QUICK NOTE

WHAT IS THE BLENDED DIET?

For people who are tube-fed (which is to say, they receive nutrition via an enteral feeding tube), the blended diet is simply food blended and given via an enteral tube as a source of nutrition, as opposed to commercial formulas.

This practice is unique to each individual and often has the oversight and support of a dietitian. The blended diet is considered a continuum, at one end some individuals may choose to give a very small amount of fruit juice or puree in combination with a commercial enteral formula, and at the other end some use blends to meet the tube-fed individual's full nutritional requirements. This allows the needs of each individual to be met in a manner which is unique to them.

If you would like to start the blended diet or require support, please reach out to a doctor or dietitian. For more information and guidelines, please visit BDA, the UK Association of Dietitians at bda.uk.com They've released a tool kit to support the blended diet practice: Practice Toolkit - The Use of Blended Diet with Enteral Feeding Tubes (Nov 2021).

DISCLAIMER

If you or your child is tube-fed, please seek the advice of your doctor or dietitian before trying any recipes herein, to ensure any recipes you would like to try meet you/your child's dietary needs and goals. If you have any concerns, please seek the advice of a medical professional.

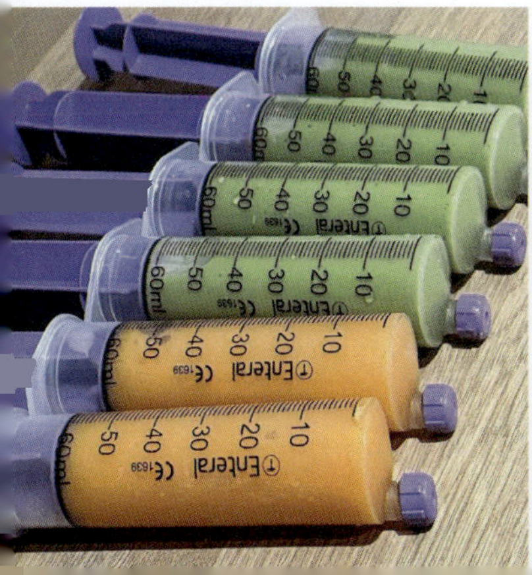

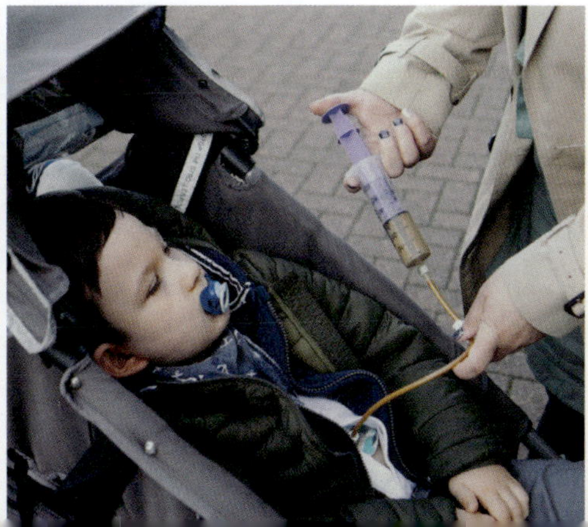

BEETS AND FETA
BLEND

Makes approx 500ml

Recipe contributed from the USA

DIRECTIONS

1. Add all ingredients to a blender. Blend until very smooth.
2. Strain through a wire mesh strainer if needed.

NOTES

Make sure the beets and carrots are soft enough that they are easily pierced with a fork, and do not undercook the quinoa or the blend is likely to become very thick!

This is a great calorie-dense blend, with just under 550kcal!

INGREDIENTS

1 cup orange juice

1 cup cooked quinoa

½ cup chopped, steamed carrots,

½ cup peeled, chopped and steamed beets

¼ cup water

3 tablespoons full fat feta cheese

1 teaspoon olive oil

1 teaspoon fresh or dried dill

PEAS AND RICOTTA
BLEND

Makes approx 400ml

Recipe contributed from the UK

DIRECTIONS

1. Add all ingredients to a blender. Blend until very smooth.
2. Strain as needed.

NOTES

A very bright blend, add more broth if you would like a thinner blend. Makes approximately 400 ml and provides around 400kcal.

INGREDIENTS

1 cup thawed frozen peas

2 tablespoons whole-milk ricotta

1 teaspoon olive oil

2 teaspoons lemon juice

1 teaspoon lemon zest

1 teaspoon fresh dill

½ cup steamed potatoes

¾ cup vegetable broth

THE EASIEST WEETBIX BLEND

BLEND

DIRECTIONS

1. In a blender, place the weetbix bar, coconut milk, honey, the pear, cored and roughly chopped, and the kiwifruit, peeled and roughly chopped, and the strawberries, hulled.
3. Pulse to get things going, and blend until smooth.

ABOUT

This is Mikaere's breakfast, most mornings. It's very flexible, you can change the fruit out as you please with whatever you have on hand (blueberries, mango, melon, and peaches are all good alternatives).

Serves 1, approx 240ml

Recipe contributed from the UK

INGREDIENTS

1 Weetbix/Weetabix bar

140ml coconut milk drink

1 teaspoon honey

½ a pear

1 kiwifruit

a handful of strawberries

AFTERNOON TEA
BLEND

Makes approx 150ml

Recipe contributed from the USA

INGREDIENTS

1 biscuit (like a Belvita biscuit, or an oatly cake)

1 teaspoon soaked chia seeds

100g baby fruit puree (apples, peaches, bananas etc)

1 tablespoon crème fraîche

DIRECTIONS

1. Add all ingredients to a blender. Blend until very smooth.
2. Strain through a wire mesh strainer if needed.

NOTES

An easy blend, better for a bullet blender rather than a big Vitamix which are better for batch blending. Contains approximately 165kcal, depending on what biscuit and fruit you add.

BANANAS + AMARANTH
BLEND

Makes 8-10oz

Recipe contributed from the USA

INGREDIENTS

1 can coconut milk

1 banana, peeled

1 cup dry amaranth, cooked and cooled

DIRECTIONS

1. Cook the amaranth according to the packet instructions.
2. Blend all ingredients until smooth, strain if needed.

NOTES

This recipe doesn't contain vegetables, but it was one of my go-to's when we were desperate for my son to gain weight. Amaranth is an ancient grain that packs a surprising caloric punch! You can easily adjust this recipe to include some vegetables (toss in some spinach!) or add more protein with cow's milk if your tubie can handle dairy. Each 8-10 ounce (225ml - 285ml) feeding contains approximately 346 calories, 17 g fat, and 7 g protein.

CARROT CAKE OATMEAL

BLEND

Makes approx 600ml

Recipe contributed from the UK

DIRECTIONS

1. Add all ingredients to a blender. Blend until very smooth.
2. Strain, if needed.

NOTES

You can sub 2 tablespoons of honey for the dates if you prefer, and both the milk and cream cheese can be substituted with plant-based alternatives if your tubie is dairy free. Also, a good trick is to add the dates to the oatmeal as it cooks, as this helps soften the dates, making them easier to blend. This recipe contains approximately 615 calories, 20g fat, and 20g protein.

INGREDIENTS

1 cup cooked oatmeal

1 cup milk

½ cup steamed carrots

2 medjool dates

2 tablespoons chopped walnuts

1 tablespoon cream cheese

1 teaspoon fresh minced ginger

1 teaspoon ground cinnamon

BUTTERNUT SQUASH RICE

BLEND

Makes 600ml

Recipe contributed from the USA

DIRECTIONS

1. Blend all ingredients until smooth. Add a small amount of water to reach the desired consistency. Strain if needed!

NOTES

You can use any long-grain rice, like jasmine rice. This recipe has approximately 615 calories, 19g fat, and 32g of protein.

INGREDIENTS

1 cup cooked basmati rice

1 cup chopped, peeled and steamed butternut squash

1 cup milk

½ cup vegetable broth

¼ cup cooked chicken breast

1 tablespoon chopped raw white onion

1 tablespoon extra virgin olive oil

¼ teaspoon ground dried sage

THE GREEN BLEND

BLEND

Makes approx 500ml

Recipe contributed from the UK

INGREDIENTS

1 courgette

¼ head of broccoli

¼ head of cauliflower

¼ steak

¼ cup couscous

½ avocado

½ green pepper

1 kiwifruit

2 prunes

4-5 snap peas

1 tablespoon walnut halves

1 tablespoon brazil nuts

1 teaspoon olive oil

1 teaspoon coconut oil

1 large bunch of coriander

½ cup water

DIRECTIONS

1. Roughly chop the courgette, broccoli and cauliflower and place in an ovenproof dish. Drizzle in olive oil, and roast at fan 180 °C/350 °F for around 30 minutes, until cooked through and soft.
2. Heat a pan with olive oil, and cook the steak till well done. Dice the cooked steak and set aside.
3. Throw your cup of couscous in a bowl, add ¼ cup of boiling water and cover with a plate to keep it warm.
4. Prep the other veg/fruit - dice the avocado and green pepper, peel and dice the kiwifruit.
5. In the blender, put the soft ingredients in first (coriander, cauliflower, avocado, courgette, kiwifruit, water) before adding everything else.
6. Pulse first, and then blend as normal. You may need to add extra water to reach the desired consistency.

NOTES

The above recipe makes approximately 570kcal, with 35g fat, 20g protein. This is a super flexible blend. It's split into four, a meat, a grain, vegetables and fats. Within that, there is freedom to add or remove ingredients as you like, or by what you have on hand. Though, if you move away from green ingredients, the less green the blend will be.

Vegetables/fruit: Roasted Courgette, broccoli, cauliflower, sweet potato, carrots, potato, beetroot, peppers, Green beans, coriander, tomatoes, kiwifruit, prunes, snap peas, sprouts etc

Grains: Couscous, quinoa or lentils, wild rice, sometimes pasta

Fats: Olive oil, coconut oil, avocado, nut butters

Meats: Steak, Ham etc

Other things, just for fun: mixed nuts (mixed/brazil/walnuts nuts), prunes, hummus, herbs or spices (paprika, turmeric etc), other interesting things from the fridge to change up the blend slightly week to week.

THE PURPLE + YELLOW BLENDS

BLEND

Makes approx 500ml

Recipe contributed from the UK

PURPLE INGREDIENTS

½ head of cauliflower

½ a medium-sized eggplant/aubergine

1 sweet potato

3 peeled + precooked beetroot

¼ **cup** cooked chicken

¼ **cup** wild rice

½ avocado

½ cup blueberries

½ cup purple grapes

2 prunes

1 teaspoon peanut butter

1 teaspoon coconut oil

½ **cup** water

YELLOW INGREDIENTS

¼ head of cauliflower

½ sweet potato

1 hearty slice of raw pumpkin, peeled

1 carrot

2 chunky slices of cooked ham

¼ **cup** quinoa

½ yellow pepper

1 tomato

2 prunes

1 teaspoon olive oil

1 teaspoon pumpkin oil

½ **teaspoon** turmeric

½ **cup** water

DIRECTIONS FOR EITHER BLEND

1. Roast the vegetables that need roasting. Chop and drizzle in olive oil, and roast at fan 180 °C/350 °F for around 20-30 minutes, until cooked through and soft.
2. Cook your grains according to the instructions on the packet, and ensure they're very well done.
3. Dice the other veg/fruit.
4. In the blender, put the soft ingredients in first before adding everything else.
5. Pulse first, and then blend as normal. You may need to add extra water to reach the desired consistency.

NOTES

The purple recipe makes approximately 580kcal, with 22g fat, 16g protein.

The yellow recipe makes approximately 550kcal, with 25g fat, 15g protein.

Like the green blend, it's split into four, a meat, a grain, vegetables and fats, and is very flexible.

INDEX

the mikaere foundation

THANKS SO MUCH FOR BEING HERE WITH US

We can't fund a cure without you, so genuinely, thank you for picking up a copy of the NKH Charity Cookbook. A few quick asks:

If you make something, we'd love to see it! Tag @mikaerefoundation and use the hashtag #nkhCharityCookbook so we can see your creations!

Please take two seconds to leave us an Amazon review. The more reviews we have, the more likely we are to sell copies, which means more funds for NKH Research. It doesn't have to be long, a quick "it's great!" works a treat.

If you spot a mistake, please let us know by emailing hello@mikaerefoundation.org. We'll make sure to fix it in the next edition. If you've got a copy with printing errors (with big white lines along the side of the pages), let Amazon know. They should replace your copy for free.

You're the best, did you know? Thank you for supporting NKH Research.

The Mikaere Foundation Team
www.mikaerefoundation.org
@mikaerefoundation